Let 'Em Talk

Oral Language Activities for the Classroom

Mary Young Williams

DALE SEYMOUR PUBLICATIONS

To Mom and Dad

who raised me in a stimulating home
of sixteen brothers and sisters.
The "meaningful noise" in that home
motivates me to seek the same
talking, sharing, and caring
in the classroom.

The author and publisher gratefully acknowledge permission to reprint the following copyrighted material:

"Ten Little Chicks" and "Sleepy Time" from *Talking Time* by Louise Binder Scott and J. J. Thompson. Copyright 1951. Reprinted by permission of Louise Binder Scott.

"Lazy Jack" from *Folk Stories* by Edward and Marguerite Dolch. Copyright 1952. Reprinted by permission of DLM Teaching Resources, a division of DLM, Inc., Allen, TX 75002.

"The Eel" and "The Guppy" from *Verses from 1929 On* by Ogden Nash. Copyright 1942, 1944 by Ogden Nash. "The Eel" first appeared in *The New Yorker*. "The Guppy" first appeared in the *Saturday Evening Post*. By permission of Little, Brown and Company.

"Arithmetic" from *The Complete Poems of Carl Sandburg*, copyright 1950 by Carl Sandburg; renewed 1978 by Margaret Sandburg, Helga Sandburg Crile and Janet Sandburg. Reprinted by permission of Harcourt Brace Jovanovich, Inc.

"Habits of the Hippopotamus" by Arthur Guiterman from *Gaily the Troubadour*, copyright 1936. Reprinted by permission of Louise H. Sclove.

Excerpt from "On the Columbia" in *Paul Bunyan*, copyright 1924, 1952 by Esther Shephard. Reprinted by permission of Harcourt Brace Jovanovich, Inc.

Excerpt from "Peculiarsome Abe" from *Abe Lincoln Grows Up* by Carl Sandburg, copyright 1926, 1928 by Harcourt Brace Jovanovich, Inc.; renewed 1954, 1956 by Carl Sandburg. Reprinted by permission of the publisher.

Editing: Deborah Kransberg
Illustrations: Mitchell Rose
Cover design: Rachel Gage

DS03702
ISBN 0-86651-360-4

DALE SEYMOUR PUBLICATIONS
P.O. BOX 10888
PALO ALTO, CA 94303

abcdefgh-MA-893210987

Acknowledgments

I wish to thank Kathy Shipley, whose hours of support and inspiration kept me on track and working toward the deadlines. Her help as a researcher, artist, and friend propelled this book toward completion.

Thanks to SuzAnne Breummer, principal of El Roble Elementary School, Gilroy Unified School District, Gilroy, California, for sharing her love for literature with me, for piloting the book with teachers, and for offering suggestions to promote oral language in all classrooms.

Thanks to Deborah Kransberg, editor, for her intense work with the revision of this book. The manila envelopes passed several times in the mail as we worked toward one goal—to bring oral language into the classroom.

Thanks to Beverly Cory, editorial director at Dale Seymour Publications, for showing me effective techniques for writing adaptations. I am also appreciative to her and to Dale Seymour for giving me this opportunity to share the belief that oral language activities can make the classroom an exciting place for thinking and speaking.

Contents

Preface

The days of silent classrooms flash before me as an uneasy memory of yesteryear, when I needed that silence to prove that I could control my class. During my first decade of teaching, I needed assurance from colleagues and administrators that "the new kid on the block" taught with enthusiasm *and* control. While wanting control, I could also see that the best lessons sprang from my enthusiastic interaction with the kids. Packaging excitement in silent bottles posed a problem until I graduated to a new level of teaching, where "noise" was no longer synonymous with "lack of control." Once I saw the value of the buzzing, bubbling talking, I came to enjoy it and embraced the happiness of learning.

Now, during my sixteenth year of teaching, I enjoy entering my classroom, where I feel safe, heard, effective, and loved. I readily label the students as "my kids." Each year I grab them by the hands, refuse to hear their stubborn whimpers of "I *can't*," and guide them through classroom experiences until they confidently release my hand and shout, "I CAN!" Those experiences must include talking, sharing, and analyzing. In my classroom, oral language skills weave throughout our activities as the core of all learning. Develop oral language skills in your classroom and you, too, will enjoy the vibrations.

Here I want to share with you, my colleagues, not only my optimistic philosophy of teaching, but also a collection of classroom-tested strategies that work. I wouldn't think of promoting "noise" in the classroom without also showing you how, why, and what to do. *Let 'Em Talk* offers you the things I myself look for in a classroom resource book. Packed with practical ideas and activities, this book prepares you for the "meaningful noise" of creative dramatics, oral interpretation, and group discussion. It provides samples from literature, helping you to create a rich language environment and to make the connection between literature and oral language. As you see the way I have adapted stories and poems for different oral language activities, you will get a sense of how to make your own adaptations from literature.

In these pages, I share with you a structured plan that underlies my teaching style. The suggestions in this book should bolster your self-confidence—and your courage to allow more talking in your classes—as you begin looking at ways to:

- set up the classroom for "meaningful noise."
- handle groups of students making such noise.
- provide a rich and safe risk-taking environment so that no student need hesitate to speak up.
- use the strategies and materials of oral language development in your daily lessons.
- establish guidelines for student roles and responsibilities in a classroom where talking is part of the learning process.

You may feel that you do not have time to teach yet another subject in an already-crowded curriculum. The fact is, you're not teaching a new subject, just developing students' oral language skills and helping them apply those skills in the content areas. We all use oral language skills every day—at home, at work, and at school. Helping your students master these skills brings your classroom closer to the real world.

I dared a number of years ago to trust my own intuition about teaching. I learned to trust that voice that tells me, "You *can* smile before Christmas!" I listen to that voice shouting, "Dare! Let 'em talk!" As long as I can show the curricular basis for my "crazy ideas," confidence in my chosen teaching style continues to blossom and grow. Now, I pass the baton to you. I urge you to trust yourself, push yourself, and enjoy yourself in your own classroom.

M.Y.W.

Introduction

Goals of the Oral Language Program

Let 'Em Talk focuses on the process of acquiring oral language skills. The broad goals of the program are as follows:

- To provide opportunities for students to enhance their self-esteem.
- To enhance students' abilities to communicate with a variety of audiences.
- To enable students to verbalize concepts.
- To help students speak coherently and in complete sentences.
- To improve students' listening skills.
- To help students become fluent in expressing feelings and opinions.
- To expose students to a variety of literary experiences.

More specific goals for creative dramatics, oral interpretation, and group discussion are listed in the corresponding sections of this book.

Why Teach Oral Language Skills?

Administrators, boards of education, and professional associations have placed increasing emphasis on oral language development. The following statements appeared in the 1979 *Handbook for Planning an Effective Reading Program*, prepared by the California State Department of Education:

> "Because oral language patterns have been shown by research to be so important as a base for reading, the framework stresses oral communication throughout all levels of the reading curriculum." (page 5)

> "Success in all aspects of language arts is dependent upon the development and extension of oral language skills. Every classroom should provide numerous opportunities for oral language practice through discussion, reporting, and question and answer sessions." (page 8)

In its 1985 Model Curriculum Standards, the California State Board of Education made this statement:

> "Schools thus cannot consider skill acquisition in speaking and listening automatic and superficial. Further, *the foundation for reading, writing, and thinking lies in the oral world* [emphasis

added]. Language carries both the content and the processes of learning; for example, teachers and other students model fair and faulty processes daily in their conversations." (page E-24)

In 1985 the California Association of Teachers of English called for the following:

"Organized activities requiring oral expression, such as discussion, reports, interviews, play-reading, and performance.

"Organized activities to develop active listening skills and the skills to relate the information acquired by the listening.

"Oral language development at all grades and ability levels.

"Curriculum to facilitate the transition of students in minority programs to programs of language fluency."

Oral language is clearly taking its rightful place at the core of learning.

Using This Book

Please do not follow this book from beginning to end! *Let 'Em Talk* is intended as a resource and idea book for teachers of grades K–8. It does, however, give you materials to put directly into the hands of students. In so doing, *Let 'Em Talk* frees you to try the process of letting kids talk in your classroom. Since the activity sheets include poems, stories, scripts, and folktales, the activities can be repeated countless times, at any grade level, simply by substituting your own favorite stories and verses.

Using the text selections on the activity sheets saves you an initial trip to the library and lets you put all your energies into trying the form, whether it's creative dramatics, oral interpretation, or group discussion. As you try the activities, freely adapt them to fit your teaching style. Then, when you feel comfortable with the activities, your creative instincts will lure you to the library where you'll find other literary selections to use with the same activity sheet. (Ah, look what's happening: your enthusiasm and ingenuity as a creative teacher dominate your lesson planning now, not a silent textbook or lifeless, fill-in-the-blanks dittos!)

Once you feel secure about the process, *Let 'Em Talk* relies on your ability to adapt any literary selection for your grade level. As you choose ideas from this guide, remember that an activity that seems best suited for younger children can easily be adapted for older students, and vice versa. At the same time, don't assume that an activity based on a fairy tale or nursery rhyme is suitable only for young children. Even at the middle school level, teenagers enjoy adapting such forms for chants, puppet shows, storytelling, readers' theater, and other presentations for younger audiences.

Divided into three sections corresponding to the sections in *Let 'Em Talk* (creative dramatics, oral interpretation, and group discussion), this diagram illustrates the variety of techniques and forms involved in oral language development.

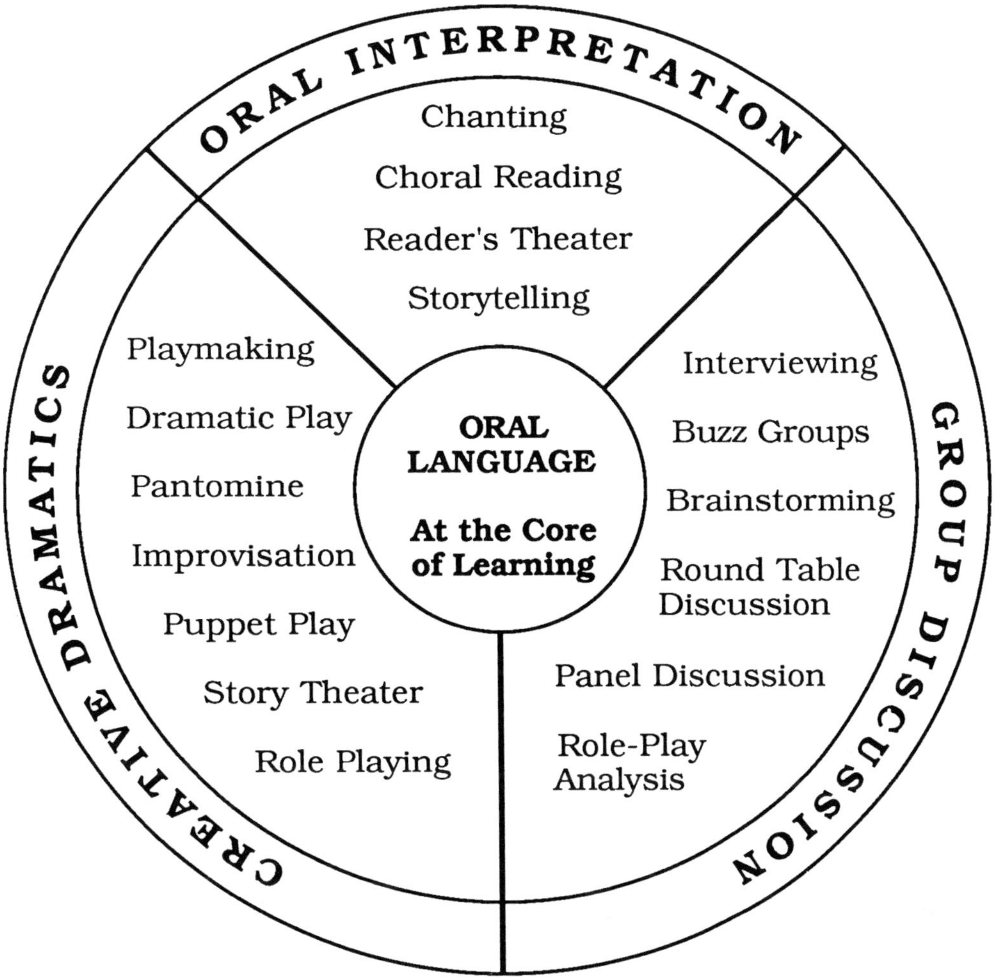

The diagram clearly shows that oral language is more than "just talking" or "making noise." Check yourself to see which terms you already know and use in the classroom. If some of the forms are totally unfamiliar to you, you are in for a treat. The guide sheets, activity sheets, and rating sheets in this book equip you to try each form and experience success.

As you use the activities in each section, be flexible enough to experiment and try overlapping techniques between sections. For example, in the oral interpretation section, a readers' theater activity on "The Three Wishes" can be extended with activities in improvisation (a creative dramatics skill) and round table discussion (a group discussion skill). Challenge yourself to mix and match activities and tap your intuitive ability to plan lessons that suit your teaching style.

To help you explore the different forms and techniques with your students, each section of the book is organized around these key features:

- **Guide Sheets.** Guide sheets were designed to address questions or concerns you might have about each oral language form. As an example, guide sheets show you the best physical arrangement of the room for different kinds of oral presentations; they introduce new terms; and they offer guidelines for making the techniques work with your students. If you wish, guide sheets can be used as student handouts to help you explain specific strategies and terms prior to an upcoming class activity.

- **Activities.** Activity sheets are the heart of this book because they are ready for you to reproduce and hand to your students. Each sheet contains these parts: directions, the activity (including a literary model, if needed), suggestions for "more to do" (with ideas for crossover between forms and between content areas), and procedures (teaching strategies). Procedures appear at the bottom of the page and can be folded back when reproducing the activity sheet for use with the students. In all cases, you are encouraged to modify and adapt the activity to suit your class.

- **Spin-Offs.** Near the end of each section, you'll find a list of spin-off activities. When you've tried a number of the activity sheets in a section, read the spin-offs and create your own activity sheet. Once in a creative mode, you'll find that you can often adapt the spin-offs in one section to make activities for another section.

- **Rating Sheets.** A set of three rating sheets for each section offers you the opportunity to involve students in the evaluation process. These sheets coax you to use evaluation as a way of maximizing student involvement in the learning process. The list of skills on the rating sheets provides a peephole through which students can actively and critically observe each other. Being trained to look at each other's performances stimulates accountability for a job well done and creates a commitment to the activity. Often, showing students the rating sheets prior to the activity helps them focus on what is expected of them so they can strive to meet those expectations.

On the first sheet, students rate themselves; on the second, they rate a classmate; and on the third, they rate their group as a whole. They use a four-category rating scale: Poor, Average, Clever, Exceptional (PACE). Students are allowed to omit their signatures on the sheets when rating their classmates and groups. Take part in the rating process with students by using the individual and group rating forms yourself. Help students keep "pace" with their own learning by seeing themselves as part of a practice environment in which they can help each other learn.

Develop PACE as a skill-building climate by talking about how students could evaluate each other more effectively. Train them to defend their evaluations. In addition to using the rating sheets, spend class time discussing the students' performances. Use the following strategies:

- At the end of each activity, discuss (as a class) the experience of working on the activity.
- Always use a positive approach when evaluating students' work. Talk about the good points first.
- When monitoring individual or group work, make specific suggestions for improvement.
- Listen carefully and coach as needed.
- Use videotaping and recording to help students see/hear themselves.
- Give students plenty of opportunities to practice.

A Final Word

Let 'Em Talk should start you on your way to a busy, productive time in the classroom. As with anything new, a few go-arounds with the activities will take the uncertainty out of doing them. If this book succeeds in its purpose, before long you will find yourself in the library, selecting books or poems and saying to yourself, "I think I'll use this one for readers' theater (or storytelling, or group discussion, or role playing)." At that point, you are well on your way to fostering "meaningful noise" in your classroom. In this venture, keep in mind a piece of advice that has helped many a teacher working with active, creative, and exuberant children:

Always behave like a duck—keep calm and unruffled on the surface, but paddle like the devil underneath.

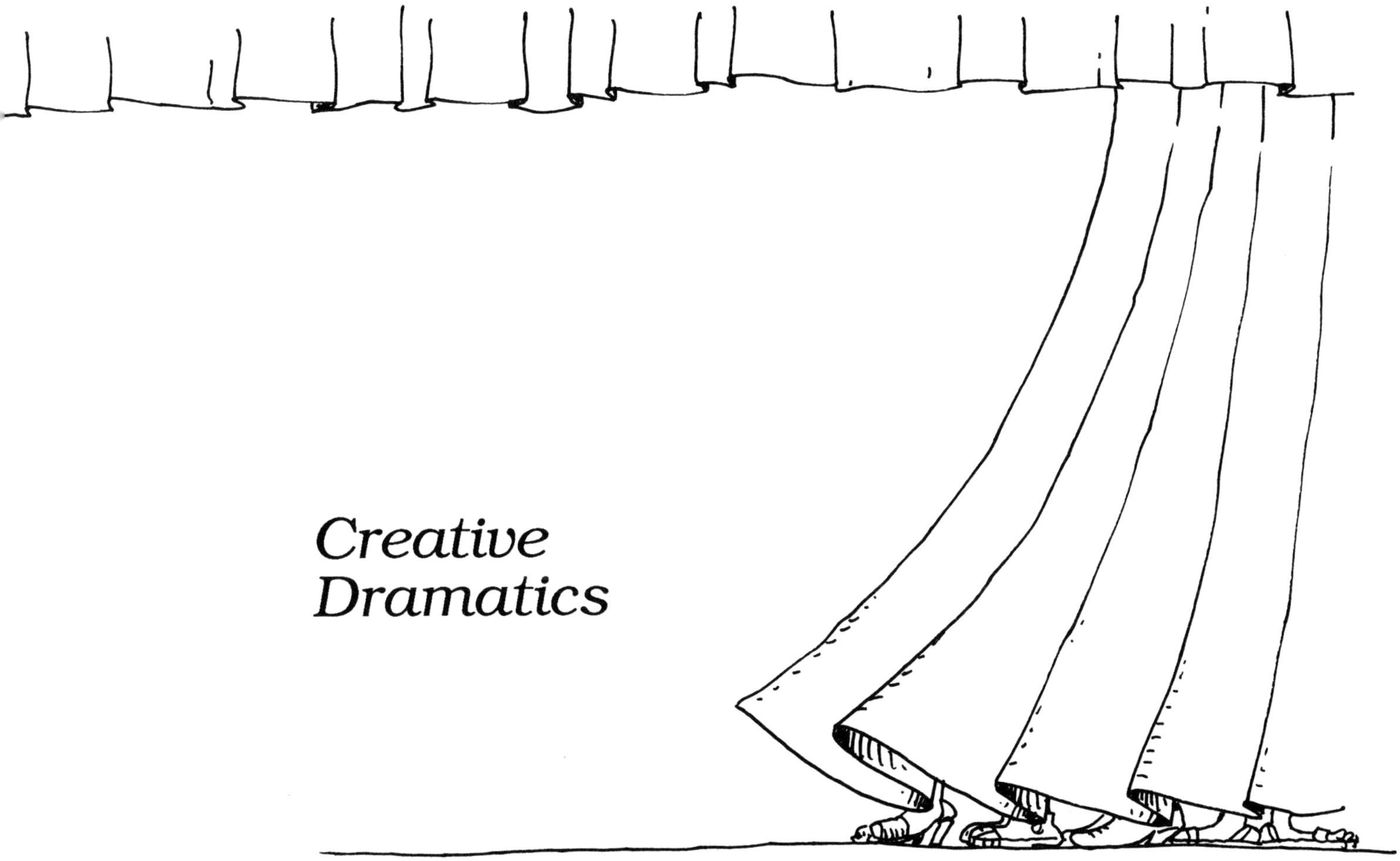

Creative Dramatics

A gesture is not sufficient.
It needs to be clothed in thought.

Jean-Louis Barrault

Getting Started in Creative Dramatics

Playing "pretend" and fantasizing sparkle in my childhood memories. Yet now, as an adult, I stand in the shadows and wonder at the naturalness of my children's play. How quickly a group of youngsters assign roles, play, and even set rules for the "game." Why is it that they know how to organize and to dramatize without adult intervention?

Whatever grade you teach, creative play will emerge in your classroom as long as you are willing to trust the naturalness of children. When using creative dramatics at the lower grades, you jiggle your classroom environment so that it resembles their real world. As children mature, the naturalness is often tucked safely away under routine and expected behavior, but it's still there. As an upper-grade teacher, your role shifts to motivator and facilitator as you set a safe stage that allows students' inherent flair for creative dramatics to emerge.

Within this section, activities progress from the spontaneity of **playmaking** to the more structured **dramatic play,** then to the decision-making and plotting processes of **pantomime** and **improvisation.** Under these umbrellas you'll discover the dramatic forms of **puppet play, role playing,** and **story theater.** Practicing these techniques gives your students a chance to play with language in an environment that is safe for creative, impromptu expression. The common thread as you progress through playmaking, dramatic play, pantomime, and improvisation is the natural fiber of "let's pretend."

Regardless of the content area, students process concepts more readily when they tap the drama within themselves. Besides sharpening listening skills, involvement with creative dramatics promotes the total physical response to learning. I know you will enjoy the active, fun-filled place your classroom becomes when you include creative dramatics in your lesson plans. See Guide Sheet 1, page 4, for more extensive descriptions of the techniques and forms of creative dramatics.

Goals of Creative Dramatics

Social Goals

The student will

- build self-confidence.
- learn group cooperation.
- develop social awareness.

Critical Thinking Goals

The student will

- listen with comprehension.
- read with comprehension.
- develop creative abilities.
- analyze poetry and stories.
- analyze familiar situations.
- analyze and solve problems.

Creative Dramatics Goals

The student will

- demonstrate comprehension by "acting out" ideas.
- be spontaneous and original.
- use voice, facial expressions, and body language.
- prepare dialogue and plots.
- use role playing to solve problems.
- coordinate active listening and dramatizations.
- use props and costumes appropriately.

Techniques and Forms of Creative Dramatics

Techniques of Creative Dramatics

Playmaking Players cooperate in spontaneous free play or "let's pretend."

Dramatic Play This more-structured play involves a sense of plot and characterization that is initiated and developed by the players themselves.

Pantomime Players act out a situation, a poem, or a story by using facial expressions and body gestures, but no dialogue.

Improvisation Players use extemporaneous pantomime and dialogue to formalize plot and characters in creative play based on given situations.

Forms of Creative Dramatics

Puppet Play This form of creative play and spontaneous dialogue lets the players hide behind puppet "masks."

Story Theater Players perform the nonverbal acting out of a poem or story as someone reads it aloud.

Role Playing Groups of players act out a problem situation, taking character roles and trying to find a solution.

Starting Creative Dramatics

These suggestions can help you get started with the creative dramatics activities.

1. Select poetry or stories that have a lot of action. You will see many action verbs.
2. Look for descriptors in the selections, too. Adjectives and adverbs add flavor to the writing and make dramatization easier.
3. Pay attention to the dialogue. Selections for story theater require very little dialogue, but dialogue would be especially significant for role playing.
4. Select interesting poems and stories. Your audience wants to be entertained. Fairy tales and other classics provide a wealth of choices.
5. Link the poem, situation, or other activity material to personal experiences you may have had.
6. Use voice intonation and body language to share the material enthusiastically.
7. Discuss the material so that you can understand characters and situations.
8. Pretend that you are part of what is happening in the selection. Say, "Let's be . . . ."
9. Close your eyes and visualize the scenes.
10. Discuss what you have just visualized. Ask members of your group, "Did you like being . . . ?"
11. Act out the scene.
12. Act out the scene again, for the practice.

Loosening Up for Creative Dramatics

Practice these activities. They are designed to help you "loosen up" before you try all the different kinds of creative dramatics.

Body Movements
Do a variety of body movements. Follow these simple commands as your teacher or member of your group gives them: jump, skip, spin around, shake, bend at the waist. Make these smaller body movements too: yawn, squint, frown, snap your fingers, shake a foot.

Body Games
Play charades and other body games such as Mother, May I?, Follow the Leader, and Simon Says.

Mirror
Pretend that a mirror is standing between you and a classmate partner. One of you makes a gesture; then the other person "follows the leader" and makes the same gesture. Change roles after a while.

Blindfold
First, rearrange some of the furniture in the classroom. Then, take turns putting on a blindfold and trying to make your way around the room.

Slow Motion
Practice these and other everyday body movements in slow motion: scratching, sitting, standing, skipping, bending, yawning.

Whose Voice?
Stand behind a closed door. Then an unidentified classmate stands on the other side of the door. As the classmate speaks, try to guess who it is by listening to the voice. Use disguised voices for a greater challenge.

Character Watch
Select a character such as a witch, ghost, old person, parent, or giant. Imitate what you think that character would say or do.

Adjectives
On cards or pieces of paper, write several "feeling" adjectives such as *angry, sad, mad, happy,* and *disappointed.* Then, pick one and pantomime the feeling the adjective expresses.

Playmaking

Definition: Spontaneous free play or "let's pretend" play that leads into creative dramatics

Activity Ideas

1. Put five different kinds of hats in the center of the room. Have students take turns trying on the hats and showing the class how they would behave while wearing them.
2. Put different kinds of shoes in the center of the room. Have students take turns selecting a shoe and pretending that they have walked a day in "someone else's shoes."
3. Hand a fistful of play money to each student in turn. Have the student show the class what he or she would do with the money if it were real.
4. Let students select either a microphone or a hoop and pretend they are on stage. What would they do with their object?
5. Provide pictures of outdoor scenes such as mountains, a desert, a parking lot, a park, an ocean or other body of water, and a sunset. Have students each select one scene and pretend they are there. What would they do?
6. Provide pictures of indoor scenes such as rooms in the house, a bus depot, a courtroom, a hotel room, and a garage. Have students each select one scene and pretend they are there. What would they do?
7. Put into a box small tools and household items, such as a screwdriver, hammer, ladle, whisk broom, feather duster, and saucepan. Have students take turns reaching into the box without looking to pick an item. Then they must show how their item would be used.
8. Give students fake eyeglasses and mustaches. Tell them to take turns showing the class the new personality that the glasses and mustaches give them.
9. Have students create unusual uses for an eraser, a pencil, chalk, a book, or another classroom item. For example, a student could use the eraser as a telephone and hold it first to his or her mouth, then ear, to carry on a "conversation" with the person on the other end of the line.
10. Provide several pictures depicting people in different careers. Have each student choose a picture and show the class how a workday in the life of this person would begin.

Dramatic Play

Definition: Play that has the dramatic elements of plot and characterization initiated and developed by the students themselves.

Activity Ideas

1. Name one historical figure; for example, Susan B. Anthony or Martin Luther King, Jr. Have students form groups to plan and present skits in which the historical figure works to solve a classroom problem.
2. Arrange part of the classroom as a kitchen, office, or other realistic setting. Divide students into groups to plan and present skits in that setting with familiar characters from books or stories they have read.
3. Have groups of students each select a plot summary from *TV Guide* and give an impromptu skit based on it. Tell students to create characters that are different from the ones in the actual TV show.
4. Have students give basic plot summaries of their favorite movies. List these plots on the board. The students then work in groups to create skits that combine some of the movie plots. As a skit is presented, ask the class to decide whether it had a clear beginning, middle, and end. Also, have students describe the plot conflict and tell how the conflict was resolved.
5. Read the opening of a short story aloud to the class, stopping after you have given them the characters, setting, and conflict. Have groups create skits to finish the story and then present the skits to the class.
6. Read an entire short story aloud to the class. Have groups decide on alternative endings for the story and present them as skits to the class.
7. Have students work in groups to make up skits based on different holidays. The holidays should not be named in the skit so that the class, when watching, can guess what holiday is being depicted.

Pantomime

Definition: The dramatization of a situation, poem, or story by means of facial expressions and body gestures, but no dialogue.

Activity Sheets

- page 10
  Old Duke of York (a poem)

- page 11
  Ten Little Chicks (a counting poem)

- page 12
  Show Us How You . . . (a list of everyday activities)

- page 13
  See a Pin (a nursery rhyme)

- page 14
  Sleepy Time (a poem)

Listen to your teacher read this poem. Chant along with the lines. Move your body to match the directions of the soldiers marching. Stand up when you hear "You're up." Stoop down when you hear "You're down."

OLD DUKE OF YORK

Oh, the grand old Duke of York,
He had ten thousand men;
He marched them up the hill,
And marched them down again.
And when you're up, you're up,
And when you're down, you're down,
And when you're only halfway up,
You're neither up nor down.

PROCEDURES: Read the poem to the entire class. Demonstrate chanting and body movements.

Listen to your classmates read this counting poem. Hold up your hands and put up all ten fingers. As each chick goes away, bend one finger down at a time.

TEN LITTLE CHICKS

by Louise Binder Scott

Ten little chicks sat under a vine.
One flew away, and then there were nine.

Nine little chicks cried, "Wait, wait, wait!"
One went to get a drink, and then there were eight.

Eight little chicks in a line so even.
One ran to get some corn, and then there were seven.

Seven little chicks said, "We're in a dreadful fix."
One said, "I'm leaving, too," and then there were six.

Six little chicks were glad to be alive.
One chased a doodle bug, and then there were five.

Five little chicks were resting on the floor.
One saw the farmer, and then there were four.

Four little chicks sighed, "Oh, dear me."
One went to roost, and then there were three.

Three little chicks grew and grew and grew.
One became a rooster, and then there were two.

Two little chicks said, "We won't run."
One changed his mind, and then there was one.

One little chick said, "This is no fun."
So he grew up . . . and then there was none.

From *Talking Time* by Louise Binder Scott and J. J. Thompson. Reprinted by permission of Louise Binder Scott.

PROCEDURES: Ask for ten volunteers to read the couplets. Model the activity for one or two couplets. Instead of finger play, the students could pantomime the actions of the chicks.

Think about doing the activities listed below. Loosen up and pantomime them in your group.

SHOW US HOW YOU . . .

- pull weeds.
- wash dishes.
- wash your hair.
- put on a pair of glasses.
- get dressed.
- play with a dog.
- change a diaper.
- drink a can of soda.
- swing a baseball bat.
- bowl.
- play soccer.
- eat pizza.

MORE TO DO

PANTOMIME/SOCIAL STUDIES
Pantomime events in history and challenge your classmates to guess what they are. (Examples: signing the Declaration of Independence, digging the Panama Canal)

PANTOMIME/SCIENCE
Pantomime how science equipment works—for example, a Bunsen burner or a battery. Or try pantomiming inventors working on their inventions—for example, the telephone or the electric light. Or you might pantomime plants and animals—for example, a growing vine, a blooming flower, or a giraffe eating. Ask classmates to guess what you are.

PANTOMIME/MATH
Pantomime math symbols (=, +, –, ×, ÷, %) and see if your classmates can tell which ones you are doing.

PROCEDURES: Divide the class into groups of three or four. Ask for volunteers to demonstrate a couple of the pantomimes. At the end of the activity, students can do some of the pantomimes for the whole class to guess. Add others if interest is high.

Your group will prepare and act out a pantomime of this nursery rhyme.

SEE A PIN

See a pin and pick it up,
All the day you'll have good luck;
See a pin and let it lay,
Bad luck you'll have all day.

MORE TO DO

CHORAL READING
The whole class can work together to do this rhyme as a choral reading. One way to do it is shown below:

1 girl:	See a pin and pick it up.
All girls:	All the day, you'll have good luck.
1 boy:	See a pin and let it lay.
All boys:	Bad luck you'll have all day.

GROUP DISCUSSION
Brainstorm with your group other things that are said to bring good or bad luck, such as finding a four-leaf clover or walking under a ladder.

PERSONAL SHARING
Tell the class about an experience you have had when good luck or bad luck played an important part. Bring to class something you have used as a good-luck piece. Talk about possible reasons why some things are considered good luck and some bad luck.

PROCEDURES: Divide the class into groups of three or four. Have the students read the rhyme for themselves. Let groups try pantomiming other familiar nursery rhymes for the whole class to guess.

The three members of your group will work as a team. Choose one person to read the poem while the other two pantomime it.

SLEEPY TIME

by Louise Binder Scott

My daddy and my mummy
Came to watch me sleep.
They tiptoed softly up the stairs,
(fingers pretending to tiptoe)
As still as they could creep.

They whispered by my bedside,
(fingers at lips)
And looked at me awhile.
I had my eyes shut tightly,
(close eyes)
But I could feel them smile.

I did not move a bit and lay
As quietly as I could keep,
Because I knew they wanted me
To be so sound asleep.
(palms together beside face.)

From *Talking Time* by Louise Binder Scott and J. J. Thompson. Reprinted by permission of Louise Binder Scott.

MORE TO DO

CHORAL READING

You might have the whole class read "Sleepy Time" in unison. Insert the refrain "Sh . . . Sh . . . still" at the end of each verse.

My daddy and my mummy
Came to watch me sleep.
They tiptoed softly up the stairs,
As still as they could creep.
Sh . . . sh . . . still.

You can also do this activity with the class divided in half. One group reads the poem in unison and the other half says the refrain.

PROCEDURES: Ask one group to perform its pantomime for the whole class. Combine pantomime with choral reading.

Improvisation

Definition: Creating dialogue and pantomime extemporaneously to formalize plot and characters in creative play based on given situations.

Activity Sheets

- page 16
  Who Says? (a list of expressive sentences)
- page 17
  On the Spot (a list of common situations)
- page 18
  The Eel (a poem)

Say these sentences the way different people would say them: a mother, a father, a teacher, a friend, a little brother, a monster, an extraterrestrial alien, and so on. Match voice, the expressions on your face, and body movements. Challenge classmates to guess the people you are imitating.

WHO SAYS?

- Go to your room.
- Who, me?
- I didn't say that!
- She is stealing second base.
- I'm running late!
- When do we eat?
- He is as slow as a snail.
- It is cold in here.
- You will get yours.
- The two waitresses crashed into each other.

MORE TO DO

IMPROVISATION/SOCIAL STUDIES
Use the same sentences, but say them the way people from history might say them. (Examples: Abigail Adams moves into the unfinished White House in 1800 and says, "It is cold in here." Benedict Arnold caught spying says, "Who, me?")

IMPROVISATION/SCIENCE
Make a thermometer "come alive" with sentences it might say. (Examples: "I am feeling *up* today." "How *low* would I sink?")

IMPROVISATION
Portray math symbols (=, +, –, ×, ÷, %) and play with words in sentences and phrases that a particular symbol might use. (Examples: A plus sign might say, "to sum it up," "in addition," or "a real plus.")

PROCEDURES: Show several ways of saying a sentence. Give all students a chance to say a few sentences in front of the class.

Your group will select one of these situations for improvisation. Practice actions and dialogue for your skit and perform it in front of the class. Use props to make it more realistic.

ON THE SPOT

mother— scared child— dentist
mother— child— curfew
catcher— big game— stolen glove
teenager— missing money
little girl— overturned tricycle
allowance— unmowed lawns
teacher— lost homework
tears— scratched face— kitten
bicycle— flat tire— busy intersection
ambulance— flashing lights— your street

MORE TO DO

IMPROVISATION/SOCIAL STUDIES
Work with two or three other students to improvise a skit in which you put people from history together in a strange setting. (Examples: George Washington and Abraham Lincoln on a subway; Joan of Arc and Florence Nightingale in a spaceship)

IMPROVISATION/SCIENCE
Improvise a group skit that combines facts from science to show cause and effect. (Examples: automobiles— exhaust— pollution; space— no gravity— floating around)

PROCEDURES: Work with groups as they practice their improvisations. Discuss the dramatizations.

Your group will work out an improvisation to dramatize this poem. Practice and then perform your skit for the class.

THE EEL
by Ogden Nash

I don't mind eels
Except as meals
And the way they feels.

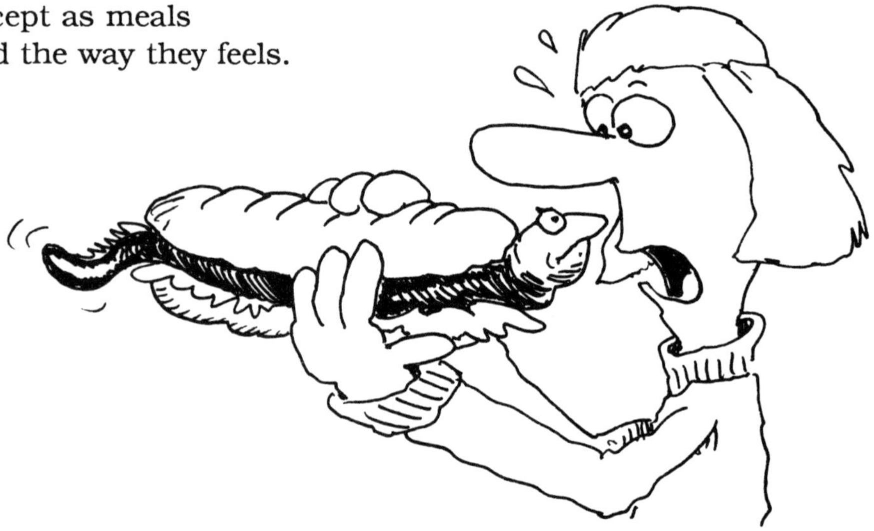

From *Verses From 1929 On* by Ogden Nash. Reprinted by permission of Little, Brown and Company.

MORE TO DO

IMPROVISATION/SCIENCE
Look up more information about the eel, such as how it looks and acts, what it eats, and where it lives. Then use improvisation to dramatize this information.

PROCEDURES: Help students find additional information. Discuss the improvisations.

Puppet Play

Definition: Creative play and spontaneous dialogue using puppets to portray characters, letting students hide behind the puppet "masks."

Activity Ideas

1. Give five animal puppets to groups of five students in turn and tell them to plan short skits using the characters. As each group presents its skit, tell the class to watch for a clear beginning, middle, and end.
2. Have students make paper bag puppets as follows: Draw and color a face, cut it out, and glue it to the bottom of a small paper bag. Put a hand in the bag along the crease and move the crease up and down to represent the mouth of the puppet. Students can work in groups to plan and present short puppet plays. These might be based on familiar stories and rhymes, or they might deal with current events.
3. Help students use socks to make puppets as follows: Shape the sock around the fingers and thumb of one hand. Sew on buttons (for eyes) and a felt tongue. Make the sock puppets talk to each other about the day's activities on the school playground.
4. Show students how to make finger puppets by using felt markers to decorate the fingers and thumb of one or both hands with tiny faces. They can use these puppets when pantomiming a counting poem. They can also pair up and make their finger puppets talk about favorite books or TV shows.
5. Students can also make "whole-hand" puppets as follows: Form the mouth by joining the pointing finger and thumb together. Draw eyes, nose, and hair on the hand to make a full face. Have students use their hand puppets to talk to each other and tell stories.
6. Have groups of students present puppet plays based on fairy tales, fables, or myths. They can use a variety of puppet types—cardboard stick puppets, sock puppets, or commercial puppets. You might insist that students follow the original plots, or you could encourage them to adapt the stories to a modern world, incorporating current slang and popular fads.
7. Have groups of students write their own scripts based on favorite reading assignments and use puppets to present their plays.

Story Theater

Definition: The nonverbal dramatization of a poem or story as it is being read aloud, usually requiring the assignment of character roles.

Activity Sheets

- page 21
  Let Us Go to the Woods (a Mother Goose rhyme)
- page 23
  The Blind Men and the Elephant (a poem)
- page 25
  Lazy Jack (a folktale)

Take turns having one student in your group read this Mother Goose rhyme while the four others take roles and pantomime to act out the words.

LET US GO TO THE WOODS

"Let us go to the woods, " says Richard to Robin,
"Let us go to the woods," says Robin to Bobbin,
"Let us go to the woods, " says John all alone,
"Let us go to the woods," says everyone.

"What to do there?" says Richard to Robin,
"What to do there?" says Robin to Bobbin,
"What to do there?" says John all alone,
"What to do there?" says everyone.

"We will catch a wren," says Richard to Robin,
"We will catch a wren," says Robin to Bobbin,
"We will catch a wren," says John all alone,
"We will catch a wren," says everyone.

"Then pounce, pounce," says Richard to Robin,
"Then pounce, pounce," says Robin to Bobbin,
"Then pounce, pounce," says John all alone,
"Then pounce, pounce," says everyone.

"She is dead, she is dead," says Richard to Robin,
"She is dead, she is dead," says Robin to Bobbin,
"She is dead, she is dead," says John all alone,
"She is dead, she is dead," says everyone.

"How shall we get her home?" says Richard to Robin,
"How shall we get her home?" says Robin to Bobbin,
"How shall we get her home?" says John all alone,
"How shall we get her home?" says everyone.

(continued on the next page)

"In a cart with six horses," says Richard to Robin,
"In a cart with six horses," says Robin to Bobbin,
"In a cart with six horses," says John all alone,
"In a cart with six horses," says everyone.

"How shall we get her dressed?" says Richard to Robin,
"How shall we get her dressed?" says Robin to Bobbin,
"How shall we get her dressed?" says John all alone,
"How shall we get her dressed?" says everyone.

"We will hire seven cooks," says Richard to Robin,
"We will hire seven cooks," says Robin to Bobbin,
"We will hire seven cooks," says John all alone,
"We will hire seven cooks," says everyone.

MORE TO DO

PANTOMIME AND CHANTING

One group can pantomime the poem while the rest of the class chants the lines. Half the chanters can say the repeating lines inside the quotation marks, and the other half can chant the "says (name) to (name)" refrain.

IMPROVISATION

Work in groups to improvise short skits that develop the characters of Richard, Robin, Bobbin, and John. Ignore the lines of the rhyme and create your own dialogue.

PROCEDURES: Remind students that they must ignore the story dialogue structure because they will not speak, just pantomime the actions.

Eight students should take turns reading the stanzas of this poem aloud while six others pantomime the actions of the blind men. Do several performances so everyone gets a chance to read and pantomime.

THE BLIND MEN AND THE ELEPHANT
by John Saxe

It was six men of Indostan
To learning much inclined,
Who went to see the Elephant
(Though all of them were blind),
That each by observation
Might satisfy his mind.

The FIRST approached the Elephant,
And happening to fall
Against his broad and sturdy side,
At once began to bawl:
"God bless me! but the Elephant
Is very like a wall!"

The SECOND, feeling of the tusk,
Cried, "Ho! What have we here
So very round and smooth and sharp?
To me 'tis mighty clear
This wonder of an Elephant
Is very like a spear!"

The THIRD approached the animal,
And happening to take
The squirming trunk within his hands,
Thus boldly up and spake:
"I see," quoth he, "the Elephant
Is very like a snake!"

The FOURTH reached out an eager hand,
and felt about the knee.
"What most this wondrous beast is like
Is mighty plain," quoth he;
"Tis clear enough the Elephant
Is very like a tree!"

(continued on the next page)

The FIFTH who chanced to touch the ear
Said, "E'en the blindest man
Can tell what this resembles most;
Deny the fact who can,
This marvel of an Elephant
Is very like a fan!"

The SIXTH no sooner had begun
About the beast to grope,
Than seizing on the swinging tail
That fell within his scope,
"I see," quoth he, "the Elephant
Is very like a rope."

And so these men of Indostan
Disputed loud and long,
Each in his own opinion
Exceeding stiff and strong.
Though each was partly in the right,
And all were in the wrong!

From *Poems* by John Godfrey Saxe (Boston: 1852).

MORE TO DO

GROUP DISCUSSION

Work in groups to talk about how people perceive things differently. Why do you think that happens? What might result from such conflicting viewpoints?

ROLE PLAYING

Use the moral of this poem to create a group script for a role-playing skit about how several of you perceive a school problem differently. How does this affect each of your solutions? Then perform your skit for your classmates.

CHORAL READING

The whole class can do this poem as a two-part choral reading. Instead of individuals reading the stanzas, let boys and girls alternate the reading.

PROCEDURES: Read the poem aloud first to familiarize the class with the vocabulary. Explain that Indostan refers to India. Have them practice the new vocabulary words before they read aloud. Instead of using a student for an elephant, it might be better to use an object (a coat draped over a desk).

Select one member of your group to read the folktale aloud. Assign the character roles: Jack, Jack's mother, farmer, baker, butcher, rich man, and rich man's daughter. Remember, use pantomime; the only voice we hear is the reader's voice.

LAZY JACK
A Folktale

Once upon a time there was a boy named Jack. He lived with his mother. His mother worked hard all of the time, but Jack was so lazy that he did not work at all. All Jack did was to play in the sun or sit by the fire and sleep. One day his mother said, "Jack, you must go to work. If you want to eat, you must work."

The day after that day, Jack went to work for a farmer. When the day was over, the farmer gave Jack some money. Jack had never had any money before, and he wanted to show it to his mother. Jack went down the road carrying the money in his hand. Before long, he lost the money. When he got home and told his mother about the money, she said, "Jack, Jack, you lost the money because you carried it in your hand. You must carry things in your pocket."

"Carry it in my pocket," said Jack. "That is what I shall do."

The day after that day, Jack went to help the farmer with his cows. When the day was over, the farmer gave Jack some milk to take home. Jack put the milk into his pocket and went down the road. When he got home, the milk was gone.

"Oh, Jack," said his mother, "you lost the milk because you carried it in your pocket. You must carry milk in a pail on your head."

"Carry it on my head," said Jack. "That is just what I shall do."

The day after that day, Jack went again to the farmer. When the day was over, the farmer gave Jack some butter to take home. Jack went down the road carrying the butter on his head. When he got home, the butter had run down all over his face and his coat.

"Jack, Jack," said his mother, "why did you carry the butter on your head? You must carry butter in your hands."

"Carry it in my hands," said Jack. "That is just what I shall do."

The day after that day, Jack went to work for a baker. When the day was over, the baker gave Jack a big black cat to take home. Jack went down the road carrying the cat in his hands. Pretty soon, a dog ran up to them and the cat jumped out of Jack's hands.

(continued on the next page)

"Oh, Jack," said the mother, "you lost the big black cat because you carried her in your hands. You must put a string around a cat and then she will walk with you down the road."

"Put a string around it; put a string around it," thought Jack, "That is exactly what I shall do."

The day after that day, Jack went to work for a butcher. When the day was over, the butcher gave Jack some meat to take home. Jack put a string around the meat and went down the road pulling the meat by the string. When he got home, his mother said, "Jack, Jack, why did you pull that meat in the road? Now we cannot eat it. If you had carried the meat on your back, it would have been good to eat."

"Carry it on my back," said Jack. "That is just what I shall do."

The day after that day, Jack went to work for a rich man. This rich man had a pretty daughter who never laughed. The rich man had said that anyone who could make his daughter laugh could have her as his wife.

When the day was over, the rich man gave Jack a little donkey.

Do you know what Jack did? He put that donkey on his back! The daughter of the rich man saw Jack going down the road with the donkey on his back. Jack looked so funny that she laughed and laughed. The rich man gave Lazy Jack his daughter as his wife. He never was lazy again.

MORE TO DO

STORYTELLING

Practice telling the story in groups, letting each member tell one part. Visualize how Jack brings home each of the things he earns. This will help you tell the story better. When your group can tell the story smoothly and dramatically, do it for the entire class.

IMPROVISATION

Work in groups to improvise skits that dramatize the story. Perform the skit for the class.

CHANTING

As one student reads the story, three students can chant "Do you know what Jack did?" every time Jack is paid for his work.

PROCEDURES: Encourage the reader to read slowly enough so that the characters can "act out" what is being read. Get Jack to exaggerate his movements. Emphasize the importance of listening. Reading *Lazy Jack* reinforces recognition of the Dolch words since this version of the story incorporates the Dolch list.

Role Playing

Definition: The dramatization of the character roles in problem situations by group members in order to clarify issues and find solutions.

Activity Sheets

- page 28
  Double Trouble (a list of problem situations)

- page 29
  In a Spot (a list of problem situations)

- page 30
  Order in the Court (a role-playing framework)

Your group will role play one of these problem situations. Your goal is to solve the problem. Prepare skits with dialogue and pantomime. Leave parts of the skit open for improvisation. Rehearse your speech, voice, and gestures so that you will sound and look realistic in your roles. Decide how you will use props.

DOUBLE TROUBLE

1. You borrowed a friend's favorite cassette tape. Yesterday your baby sister smeared peanut butter all over it after you left it on a chair. You have to return the tape today. What do you do?
2. You take your little brother with you to the roller rink. He is running all over the rink screaming and kicking the skaters. You see a friend, but you hide behind a post because you are embarrassed. What do you do?
3. When you come home from school, you see a three-layer chocolate cake on the kitchen counter. After cutting a huge piece for yourself, you flop down to watch TV. Then your mother phones and tells you that she has to rush home from work to pick up the cake for a surprise birthday party for her secretary. She asks you to put the cake in a box she left for it on top of the refrigerator. What do you do?
4. You promised your father that you would save half your weekly allowance of $5. You agreed not to spend the savings unless you receive permission from him. Yesterday you took the $110 you had saved and bought a tape recorder. Your aunt calls your father to borrow $100 because of an emergency in the family. Your father doesn't have the money so he tells your aunt that he will borrow the money from your savings account. What do you do?

MORE TO DO

PUPPET PLAY

Make up group role-playing skits that can be done with puppets. Use problem situations that are related to school.

ROUND TABLE DISCUSSION

Get into groups of five and discuss other problems and "What do you do?" strategies. Share these with the class. See how many more solutions the class can generate for each problem situation.

PROCEDURES: Have one student in each group read the situation aloud for the others. Help groups with their skit preparation and role playing as needed.

Your group will role play one of these problem situations. Your goal is to solve the problem. Prepare skits with dialogue and pantomime. Rehearse so that your speech, voice, and gestures will sound and look realistic in your roles. Dramatize your skit in front of the class.

IN A SPOT

1. You watch your best friend take a candy bar from the store shelf. Just when you are ready to talk to her, a security officer walks up to both of you. What do you do?
2. You arrive home from a party two hours late. When you open the door, you see stern looks on the faces of your mother and father. What do you do?
3. You have looked everywhere for your new watch. Your mother comes into your room carrying the watch with its face smashed. What do you do?
4. Every day after school, your two best friends have been trying to convince you to take pills to feel "high." They say they won't be friends with you unless you join in. What do you do?
5. A boy at your lunch table begins throwing peas. Soon there's a "war of peas" between two tables. Just when you decide to join in the "war," the school principal arrives and points at you. What do you do?

MORE TO DO

ROLE PLAYING AND PANEL DISCUSSION
Select a single problem that everyone agrees on and have five groups role play that same problem. Watch for different outcomes. After the performances, each group lists its reasons for solving the problem as it did. Choose one member of each group to be on a panel that discusses the reasons for the different solutions.

PROCEDURES: **After the panel discussion, have students select the solution they consider to be the best and explain why.**

Your group will role play a courtroom drama. Within your group, decide who will play the following character roles. Select one of the problem situations and practice the courtroom drama until your group is ready to present it to the entire class. Use props and costumes.

ORDER IN THE COURT

Character Roles

Judge

Principal, the one who makes the charge– the prosecution

Student who caused the problem – the defense

Lawyer for the prosecution

Lawyer for the defense

Student or teacher who tried to stop the problem– first witness

Another witness

Problem Situations

Throwing cooked carrots in the cafeteria

Pushing on the school playground

Hiding the basketball

Throwing pencils at the ceiling in class

Stealing lunch money

Making buzzing noises while the teacher is talking

Cheating on a test

Turning homework in late

MORE TO DO

BRAINSTORMING AND ROLE PLAYING

Work in groups to compile a list of problem situations that arise at home. Then role play courtroom dramas for some of those situations. Model the skits after the TV show, *People's Court.*

BUZZ GROUPS/SOCIAL STUDIES

Working in groups, use a chapter in a government, history, or other social studies book to make lists of problem situations. Each group should select one problem and list possible solutions.

PROCEDURES: Set up the classroom for the courtroom dramatizations. Instruct the class to act as the jury. Discuss afterwards.

Spin-Offs

Pantomime

- Get to know your students better by asking them to pantomime some of their favorite activities.
- Have older students go to a primary grade classroom and use pantomime to "tell" fairy tales, challenging the younger children to guess the names of the tales. Younger students can pantomime nursery rhymes for classmates to guess.

Improvisation

- Have students improvise telephone conversations between characters who disagree on a subject; for example, the ideal length of the school day, the advantages of using computers, or the social value of rock music.
- Let students improvise skits about great moments in modern American history: the first moon landing, the Voyager flight around the world, a summit meeting between Soviet and American leaders, and so on.

Puppet Play

- Have students use puppets to present skits about events in their own lives. Children will often reveal more about themselves when they can speak through puppet characters.
- Show students how to use hand puppets to perform shadow plays. Invite other classes to watch the performances.

Story Theater

- Students can write short poems or stories about themselves for story theater. Let them videotape the performances.
- Students can bring some of their favorite books, stories, and poems to class and exchange them with each other. They can then work in groups to use some of the new-found literature for story theater.

Role Playing

- Have students brainstorm lists of problems that are relevant to them. Select one of the problems and assign it to four groups to role play possible solutions. Students should then compare and contrast the four different outcomes of their enactments. Invite discussion about the need to seek several solutions to a problem.
- Bring newspapers to the classroom and have students find articles that deal with national or state issues, then work in groups to prepare role-playing skits offering possible solutions. They could also improvise their skits.
- Clip letters to the editor from newspapers to distribute to small groups. Ask one member of each group to summarize the problem in its letter. Then have groups use role playing to dramatize the problems and come up with some solutions. Discuss the various outcomes.

Your Name ______________________________ Date ______________

P = Poor
A = Average
C = Clever
E = Exceptional

RATE YOURSELF
Find your creative dramatics PACE rating.

GROUP WORK: You . . .	P	A	C	E
cooperated with everyone.				
followed and offered suggestions.				
followed directions.				
took part in planning.				
performed when called upon.				
gave others their turns to perform.				
didn't upstage others.				
helped others with problems.				

GETTING READY: You . . .	P	A	C	E
prepared realistic dialogue.				
worked out pantomime that fit.				
thought through ideas for improvisation.				
developed good plots.				
developed good characterizations.				
took part in casting performances.				
practiced.				

PERFORMING: You . . .	P	A	C	E
followed the poem, story, or situation.				
communicated roles by performing realistically.				
used body gestures that fit.				
fit facial expressions to emotions.				
fit voice pitch, intonation, and rhythm to roles.				
adjusted to the action as it unfolded.				
kept good eye contact with the audience.				
handled props and costumes well.				

Comment on what you did best in creative dramatics.

Comment on what was hardest for you.

What changes would you make the next time ?

Classmate's Name ______________________ Date ____________

RATE A CLASSMATE
Find the creative dramatics PACE rating for a classmate in your group.

P = Poor
A = Average
C = Clever
E = Exceptional

GROUP WORK: This classmate . . .	P	A	C	E
cooperated with everyone.				
followed and offered suggestions.				
followed directions.				
took part in planning.				
performed when called upon.				
gave others their turns to perform.				
didn't upstage others.				
helped others with problems.				
GETTING READY: This classmate . . .				
prepared realistic dialogue.				
worked out pantomime that fit.				
thought through ideas for improvisation.				
developed good plots.				
developed good characterizations.				
took part in casting performances.				
practiced.				
PERFORMING: This classmate . . .				
followed the poem, story, or situation.				
communicated roles by performing realistically.				
used body gestures that fit.				
fit facial expressions to emotions.				
fit voice pitch, intonation, and rhythm to roles.				
adjusted to the action as it unfolded.				
kept good eye contact with the audience.				
handled props and costumes well.				

Comment on what your classmate did best in creative dramatics.

Comment on what seemed hardest for your classmate.

What changes would you suggest the next time?

Your name ______________________

CREATIVE DRAMATICS
Rating Sheet 3

Names of Group Members

Date ____________________

______________________ ______________________

______________________ ______________________

______________________ ______________________

P = Poor
A = Average
C = Clever
E = Exceptional

RATE YOUR GROUP
Find your creative dramatics PACE rating.

GROUP WORK: The group members. . .	P	A	C	E
cooperated with everyone.				
followed and offered suggestions.				
followed directions.				
took part in planning.				
performed when called upon.				
gave others their turns to perform.				
didn't upstage others.				
helped others with problems.				

GETTING READY: The group members . . .	P	A	C	E
prepared realistic dialogue.				
worked out pantomime that fit.				
thought through ideas for improvisation.				
developed good plots.				
developed good characterizations.				
took part in casting performances.				
practiced.				

PERFORMING: The group members . . .	P	A	C	E
followed the poem, story, or situation.				
communicated roles by performing realistically.				
used body gestures that fit.				
fit facial expressions to emotions.				
fit voice pitch, intonation, and rhythm to roles.				
adjusted to the action as it unfolded.				
kept good eye contact with the audience.				
handled props and costumes well.				

Comment on what your group did best in creative dramatics.

Comment on what was hardest for your group.

What changes would you make the next time?

Your name ____________________

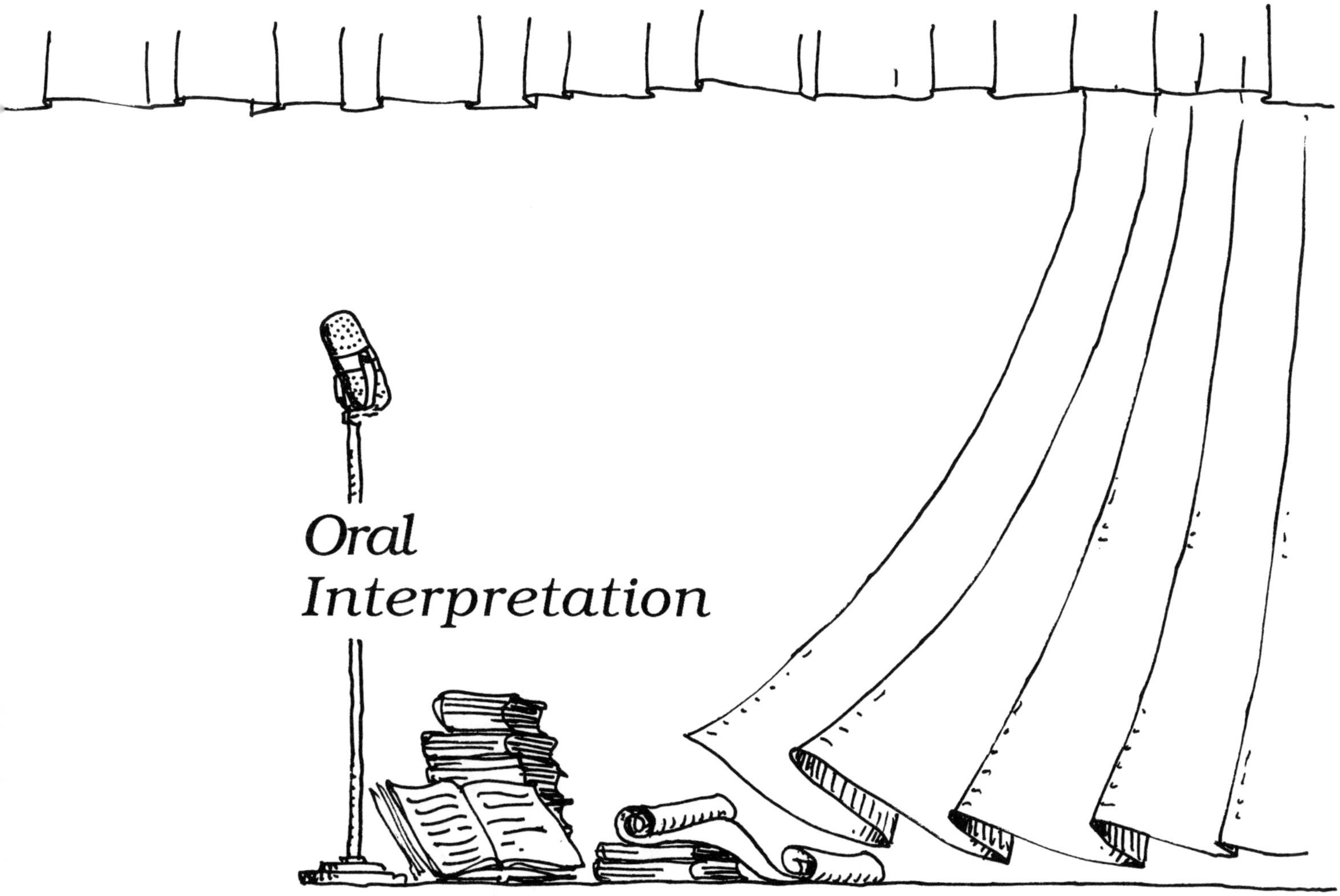

Oral Interpretation

A word is dead
when it is said,
some say.
I say it just
begins to live
that day.

Emily Dickinson

Getting Started in Oral Interpretation

I remember those deadly days. The teacher's gaze darted around the room as, pointing a finger, she assigned paragraphs to be read aloud. I skimmed quickly over and over my reading section, neither hearing nor caring about the others. My own private panic bubbled up inside me, "Please, just this once, let me read aloud without mispronouncing, skipping, or stuttering!" Don't even ask about comprehension! Actually, an even greater terror sprang from the surprise-attack approach: one of us read aloud until the teacher boomed "Stop!" while the rest of us avoided eye contact and hovered closer to our desktops, praying we wouldn't be the next victim. Alas, no prereading time, just time for sputtering and courageous attempts to sound in control!

While "reading aloud" occurred in both instances, oral interpretation did not. Blindly, students trudged through the mechanics of reading, plugging in phonics and sight words as best they could. Literature deserves far more than that! Literature begs for interpretation, begs the instrument of voice to breathe life into the printed page and bring word images into the oral/aural world. Indeed, with most literature, words should be heard and not just seen!

Breathing life into literature requires CPR: Confidence, Prereading, and Rehearsal. Oral interpretation focuses both on the *act of reading* and the *power of the human voice;* it involves phrasing, intonation, pronunciation, enunciation, projection, and pacing. Standing in the center of the training arena, you first model for your students the different forms of oral interpretation: **chanting, choral reading, readers' theater,** and **storytelling.** Students then need the chance to rehearse. Give them plenty of practice time: let 'em talk!

Reading aloud to your class carries with it so many valuable side effects: hearing excellent language models, developing a sense of story, opening thematic topics for discussion, bonding the class together, and creating a mood. Research supports these statements, but beyond that, think about your own personal feelings when someone reads to you. I know you like it! The greatest fallacy of oral language is the assumption that only primary students need it. Wrong! We all enjoy hearing language, and we all need it.

Open the doors of this read-aloud world to your students. Enjoy the process of selecting literature, absorbing the sound of literature, and interpreting and performing that sound for one another. Bring your textbooks to life through oral interpretation forms. You'll see concepts spring from the pages to be heard, enjoyed, and understood by your students. Allow chanting, choral reading, readers' theater, and storytelling into your classroom to stir up the "words in print."

In this section, you will find a variety of ways to incorporate oral interpretation into your classroom routines. For further descriptions of the forms of oral interpretation, see Guide Sheet 1 on page 40.

Goals of Oral Interpretation

Social Goals

The student will

- learn teamwork.
- develop self-esteem.
- appreciate the satisfaction of sharing with others.
- demonstrate confident self-expression.
- enjoy a positive interaction with literature.

Critical Thinking Goals

The student will

- read critically.
- listen critically.
- interpret reading materials for performance.
- learn sequencing skills.
- visualize story parts.
- develop creative planning, writing, and speaking skills.

Oral Interpretation Goals

The student will

- prepare or select suitable materials.
- perform with enthusiasm.
- increase speaking and oral-reading skills.
- develop voice, facial expression, and body language.
- use props and costumes appropriately.
- respond to an audience.

Forms of Oral Interpretation

Chanting

The repetition by a group of key phrases and expressions in the reading material, usually speaking in unison and in voices that express the actions, moods, and emotions of the words.

Choral Reading

The orchestration of voices in a chorus of readers who "sing" the language of literature instead of songs. Their voices are organized by tone: light (high), medium, and dark (deep). The reading text used should sound "good to the ear"; that is, it needs strong rhythms and rhyme patterns.

Readers' Theater

The group presentation of a script in play form, by reading rather than memorizing the lines. Primary emphasis is on putting drama into the reading. The stage is set with a few chairs that the readers can sit on or use to suggest other objects, such as a car or a boat. The readers communicate changes of scenes by means of body positions—for example, facing the wall when they "leave."

Storytelling

A way of sharing the word pictures of literature with an audience by retelling a story. Storytellers usually select stories that have repetitive phrases and exciting plots; often they choose cumulative tales. The success of storytelling is based on the standards of good oral communication: appropriate intonation, expressive body movements, and steady eye contact with the audience.

Methods of Choral Reading

Choral Refrain — Single speakers read the main parts, and the whole group joins in for the chorus or refrain.

Two-Part Work — Two groups alternate the reading of stanzas or lines. The material you use should contain questions and answers, appeals and responses, or opposing ideas.

Unison — The whole group reads together with accuracy and unity of voices and purpose.

Multiple-Part Work — All three methods (choral, two-part, and unison) are combined in any variety of ways.

Diagrams for Arranging Choral Readers

Think about your tone of voice. Is its pitch light (high), medium, or dark (deep)? These five diagrams show different ways to arrange voices by tone for choral reading.

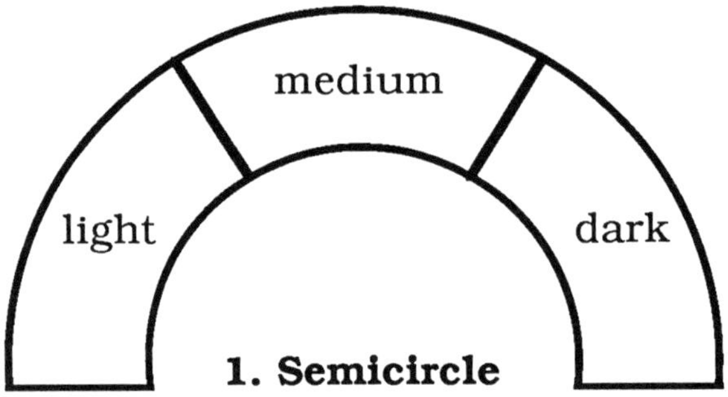

1. Semicircle

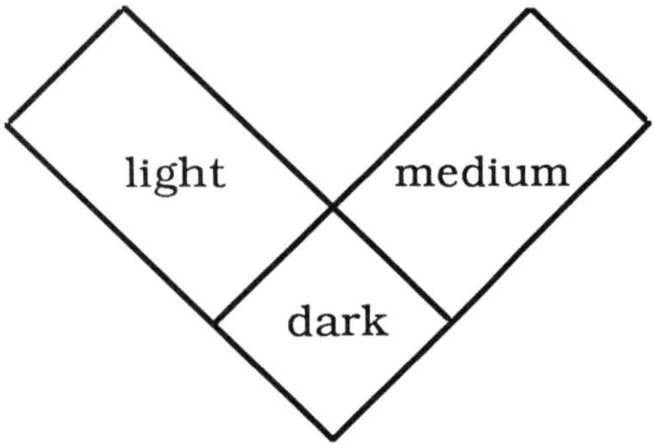

2. V formation

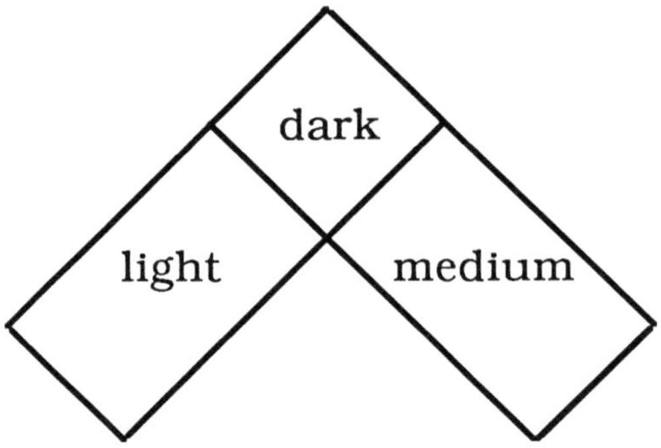

3. Inverted V

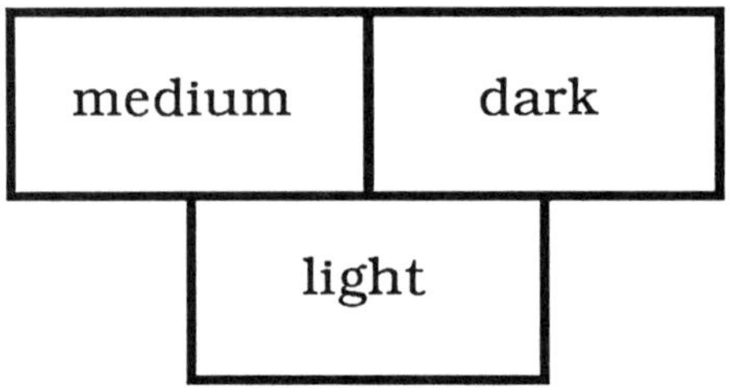

4. T formation

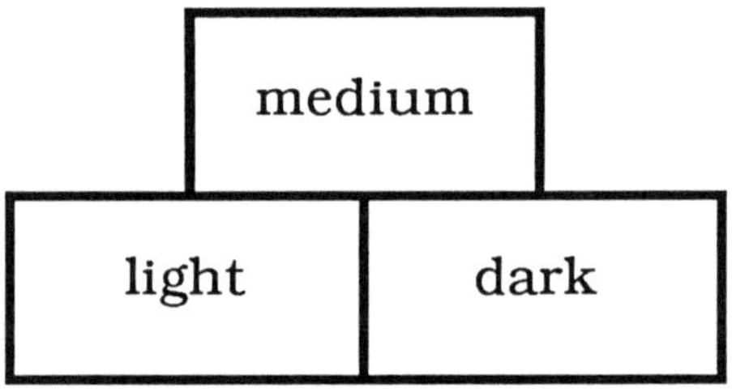

5. Inverted T

Starting Choral Reading

1. Select materials that you think would "sound good" because of their rhythm or rhyme. Use nursery rhymes to warm up.
2. Find materials that have the same theme or are the same type (serious, humorous, persuasive, and so on).
3. Mark where you would like to pause when reading aloud by using slashes (/).
4. Alter the tone of your voice while you read by changing pitch levels (light, medium, and dark). Write your instructions for pitch levels by using these symbols:

   < Voice goes up.

   > Voice goes down.
5. Mark where you would like your voice to glide over words by using equal signs (=).
6. Select words or groups of words you would like to emphasize. Assign them to single speakers, small groups, or the whole group.
7. Practice the pronunciation of difficult words to be sure you know how to say them.
8. Decide on the "beat" you want to create and practice it.
9. Practice matching your voice to the mood of the reading.
10. Decide what facial expressions, body gestures, and degree of eye contact will fit the mood of the reading.
11. Plan how to position the readers (see Oral Interpretation Guide Sheet 3).
12. Plan the physical arrangement of the room.

Preparing Poetry for Readers' Theater

1. Select poetry that could be converted into dialogue and would sound better with a variety of voices.
2. Look for unusual poetry that would entertain because of its humor.
3. Find poetry that has interesting rhymes and rhythms.
4. Avoid poetry that is heavy with allusions or metaphors since your audience may have trouble understanding the poem's meaning.
5. Avoid sight poetry, or concrete poetry, since its power depends on its visual impact, and you want to give an oral interpretation.
6. Find a variety of poetry. Use poems ranging from Shel Silverstein's "The Dirtiest Man" to Shakespearean sonnets.
7. Think of unusual ways you would like to "speak" the poem. Experiment with different tones of voice.
8. Read a poem through a few times before assigning parts. Ask group members to volunteer to read. Pick the better readers to read the narrator and multiple-line parts. Ask members who are really nervous to read the one-line parts.
9. Before presenting your poetry reading to classmates, hold a quick rehearsal. Do not overproduce the poetry.
10. Look at this sample script for poetry reading.

Jack, be nimble!	*All:*	Jack*
Jack, be quick!	*Girls:*	Be nimble!
Jack, jump over	*All:*	Jack
the candlestick!	*Boys:*	Be quick!
	All:	Jack
	Girls:	Jump over the candlestick!

**Read "Jack" by whispering or shouting.*

Preparing Stories for Readers' Theater

Here are some steps to follow to get stories ready for readers' theater.

1 Go to the library, use your literature anthologies, or use textbooks to find selections you can adapt into scripts.

2. Find stories that have repetitive phrases, plenty of dialogue and characterization, and interesting story lines. To practice, begin with shorter stories and progress to longer, more complex ones.

3. Before you change story dialogue into script, read the sample on page 46.

4. Practice "playing with the script." A technique you might use would be to have one person speak one line, three people the second line, and the whole cast the next line.

5. Think of expressive movements or actions you could include to develop characterization and add emphasis to your presentation.

Changing Story Dialogue into a Script

Before you start writing your own scripts, study this sample.

Story Dialogue

As Nicole turned the corner, she saw the pet store owner grab her kitten.

"Hey, mister," she called. "That's my kitty. I'll take her home."

"No, you won't," answered the owner. "She's mine now."

Nicole pleaded, "Oh, please, don't take my kitty. She's mine."

"She doesn't have a collar. She's mine now!" snapped the owner.

Marking Your Own Script

Narrator: As Nicole turned the corner, she saw the pet store owner grab her kitten.

Nicole: Hey, mister, ~~she called~~. That's my kitty. I'll take her home.

Owner: No, you won't, ~~answered the owner~~. She's mine now.

Nicole: ~~Nicole pleaded,~~ Oh, please, don't take my kitty. She's mine.

Owner: She doesn't have a collar. She's mine now! ~~snapped the owner~~.

Final Script

Narrator:	The setting is a street in Boston. As Nicole turns the corner, she sees that the pet store owner has just collared her kitten, Sheba.
Nicole:	Hey, mister. That's my kitty. I'll take her home.
Owner:	No, you won't. She's mine now.
Nicole:	Oh, please, don't take my kitty. She's mine.
Owner:	She doesn't have a collar. She's mine now!

Diagrams for Positioning Readers

These are just a few ways you might position readers to perform readers' theater. Readers can either sit or stand, and they can hold the reading material or rest it on a music stand. Choose what suits the story or poem you are working with. (In the diagrams, arrows show directions for eye contact with the audience.)

Two Readers

Four Readers

Many Readers

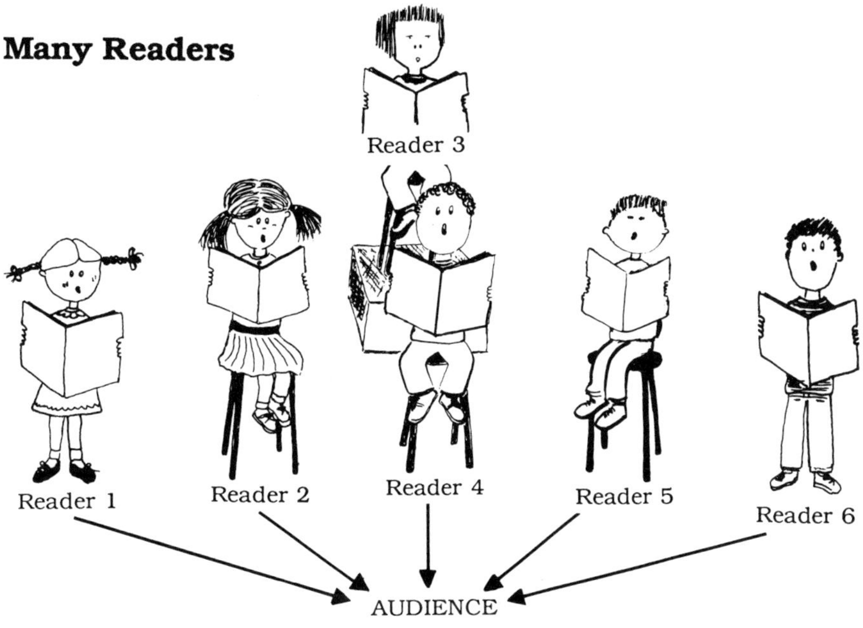

Diagrams for Arranging the Classroom

These are just a few ways you might arrange stools, music stands, and platforms for readers' theater. Make arrangements to suit the story or poem you are reading.

Two Readers

(a)

(b)

Four Readers

(a)

(b)

Many Readers

(a)

(b)

Starting Storytelling

1. Use these guidelines to select an appropriate story to tell.
   - Pick a story that fits your audience and the occasion.
   - Pick a story YOU like because of its message, mood, plot, or characterization. You will tell it better if you like it because suitable eye contact, voice, and gestures will come naturally.
   - Pick a story that will be interesting to your audience because of its realistic characterizations, strong plot, or clever humor.
   - Pick a story that will get your audience involved by enlightening, amusing, inspiring, or persuading them.
2. Read your story carefully to yourself several times to get the feeling of mood, setting, and characters. Then read it aloud several times to help you visualize the sequence of events.
3. As you read aloud, decide what parts could be omitted because they do not contribute to the story's movement.
4. Do not memorize the story. After you visualize the sequence of events, write the key words and phrases of this sequence on a note card. Practice telling this sequence.
5. Use note cards to block out and organize your presentation. Follow these suggestions:

Note Card 1	**Note Card 2**	**Note Card 3**	**Note Card 4**
·Author ·Title ·Background data about author ·Setting and culture of story	Key words and phrases of sequence of events	Names of characters and places	Key words and phrases to use when telling story

6. Practice telling the story in your own words. Use a tape recorder and practice in front of a mirror. To help you overcome your fear of an audience, practice in front of relatives and friends.
7. Practice telling the story in a small classroom group. Ask your classmates to offer suggestions for inflection, word usage, body movements, timing, and natural rhythm.

Making a Story Come Alive

As a storyteller, you want your listeners to experience the excitement, the sorrow, the anger, and the joy of the story. Here is a list of techniques a good storyteller uses to make a story come alive.

Think about your body language . . .

- Don't be self-conscious. Put yourself completely into the story and forget about yourself.
- Keep good eye contact with your listeners.
- Stand relaxed and let your body express the mood of the story.
- Use hand gestures and exaggerated facial expressions.

Listen to your voice . . .

- Use a conversational tone. Speak to your listeners as if you were talking to a good friend.
- Slow down! When people are nervous, they often talk too fast.
- Keep your voice loud enough so that everyone can hear you.
- Avoid letting your voice trail off at the end of sentences.
- Show emotion in your voice. Try to vary the volume, the pitch, and the intensity of what you are saying—not just when characters are speaking, but also during narrative parts.
- Use pauses for emphasis and to show doubt, surprise, or disbelief.

Think about your word choice . . .

- Use colorful words and action words. That is, don't just say "he went" if you can say "he scampered," and don't just say "dog" if you can say "flea-bitten mongrel."
- Use the same verb tense all the way through the story. Most books are written in the past tense, and that works for storytelling, too. Try the present tense to make it seem that your story is happening as you tell it.
- Choose a point of view and keep it the same throughout. That is, people usually tell "Little Red Riding Hood" in the third person, from the point of view of an observer. You could tell it in the first person, though, from the point of view of Little Red Riding Hood herself. Just don't switch in the middle of the story, or you will confuse your listeners.
- Avoid starting every sentence with words such as "So," or "Well," or "And then."

And generally . . .

- Keep control of the story plot. Don't get sidetracked.
- Enjoy yourself!

Chanting

Definition: The repetition by a group of key phrases and expressions in the reading material, usually speaking in unison and in voices that express actions, moods, and emotions.

Activity Ideas

1. As a warm-up activity to introduce students to chanting and get them accustomed to using their voices, have them practice saying tongue twisters. First, let them say some of the twisters alone. Then have them get into pairs to plan a chanting routine with some of them. Here are a few tongue twisters they could use.

   Shy Sally saw six Swiss wristwatches.
   She sells seashells, shellfish, and sand shoes.
   The sun shines on shop and stop signs.
   Savor the flesh of freshly fried flying fish.
   Round and round the rugged rocks the ragged rascal ran.

2. Have students read through several fairy tales and list the repetitive phrases in each. For example, in "The Three Little Pigs," they would list the following:

   Little pig, little pig, let me come in.
   Not by the hair of my chinny, chin, chin.
   I will huff; I will puff; I will blow your house down.

   You could also include this from the Walt Disney classic:

   Who's afraid of the big, bad wolf, the big, bad wolf, the big, bad wolf?

   As one student reads a tale aloud, the rest of the class chants the repetitive phrases at the appropriate points.

3. Many Mother Goose rhymes are intended to be chanted, with hand clapping to accompany the rhythms. Let students select some that would be effective done this way. Here are two.

   Pease porridge hot,
   Pease porridge cold,
   Pease porridge in the pot
   Nine days old.

   Ring around the rosie,
   A pocket full of posies,
   Hush, hush, hush,
   We'll all tumble down.

4. Work with the book *Drummer Hoff* by Barbara Emberley. Have the class chant the rhyming lines with you. Tell them to clap to the rhythm of "DrummerHoff (clap, clap) fired it off! (clap, clap, clap)."

5. Have students read aloud the lyrics of a song that has repetitive phrases for chanting. Make sure they *read*, not sing, the lyrics.

Choral Reading

Definition: The orchestration of voices in a chorus of readers who "sing" the language of literature.

Activity Sheets

- page 53
  The Camel's Complaint (a poem)
- page 55
  Days of the Week (a Mother Goose rhyme)
- page 56
  The Guppy (a poem)
- page 57
  The Fox and the Crow (a fable)
- page 58
  Arithmetic (a poem)
- page 60
  The Donkey (a poem)

Practice doing this two-part choral reading. First, girls and boys should practice their parts separately; then put the parts together.

THE CAMEL'S COMPLAINT
by Charles Carryl
Adapted for choral reading by Mary Young Williams
G = girls *B = boys*

Narrator: "The Camel's Complaint," a poem by Charles Carryl

G: Canary birds feed on sugar and seed;
Parrots have crackers to crunch.
And, as for the poodles,
They tell me the noodles
Have chicken and cream for their lunch.
B: But, there's never a question
About my digestion—
ANYTHING does for me!

G: Cats, you're aware, can repose in a chair;
Chickens can roost upon rails;
Puppies are able to sleep in a stable,
And oysters can slumber in pails.
B: But no one supposes
A poor Camel dozes—
ANY PLACE does for me!

G: Lambs are enclosed where it's never exposed,
Coops are constructed for hens;
Kittens are treated to houses well heated,
And pigs are protected by pens.
B: But a Camel comes handy
Wherever it's sandy—
ANYWHERE does for me!

(continued on the next page)

G: People would laugh if you rode a giraffe,
Or mounted the back of an ox.
It's nobody's habit to ride on a rabbit,
Or try to bestraddle a fox.
B: But, as for a Camel, he's
Ridden by families—
ANY LOAD does for me!

G: A snake is as round as a hole in the ground,
And weasels are wary and sleek;
And no alligator could ever be straighter
Than lizards that live in a creek.
B: But a Camel's all lumpy
And bumpy and humpy—
ANY SHAPE does for me!

From *The Admiral's Caravan*, by Charles Carryl (Boston: Houghton Mifflin, 1897).

MORE TO DO

GROUP DISCUSSION/GEOGRAPHY
First look in geography books, in magazines like *National Geographic*, and in encyclopedias for more information about the geographical areas where camels live in Africa and Asia. Then, in small groups, talk about what you learned from your research. Why is the camel very important to the life in these areas?

GROUP DISCUSSION/SCIENCE
Working in small groups, make a list of characteristics of the camel mentioned in the poem. Add to your list other information you find in science books, magazines, and encyclopedias. How do these characteristics help the camel survive in the desert?

STORYTELLING
List the theme or main topic of each stanza in the poem (what animals eat, where they sleep, and so on). Then retell the poem as a story, covering all the topics one by one. Use the same pattern to tell a story about another kind of animal.

IMPROVISATION
Work in groups to do an improvisational skit of the poem. Each time a new animal is introduced, pause long enough to dramatize some other characteristics of that animal.

PROCEDURES: Arrange each group by voice tone. Have the whole class read in unison or set the poem up for choral refrain, assigning a different reader for each stanza, with the whole class reading the "ANY" lines.

Read this Mother Goose rhyme. Then create a two-part choral reading script for it. Find ways to divide the whole class into two groups other than the standard division of boys/girls. Include stage directions that tell how to say the lines. The sample below can help you get started.

DAYS OF THE WEEK

Monday alone,
Tuesday together,
Wednesday we walk
When it's fine weather.
Thursday we kiss,
Friday we cry,
Saturday's hours
Seem almost to fly.
But of all the days in the week
We will call
Sunday, the rest day,
The best day of all.

SAMPLE SCRIPT

Narrator:	"Days of the Week," a Mother Goose rhyme
Group 1:	Monday*(whispering)* alone,
Group 2:	Tuesday*(deep, demanding)* together,
Group 1:	Wednesday*(whispering)* we walk *(joyfully)* when it's fine weather.
Group 2:	Thursday*(softly)* we kiss,*(and so forth)*.

PROCEDURES: The poem might also be set up so that the whole class says the days of the week for a choral refrain and groups alternate with the rest of the line. Have students work in small groups and share their scripts with the class. Give each group an overhead transparency on which to copy the script so that the class can follow along.

Work with your group to practice the choral reading version of this poem. Assign single speakers to read the main parts. The whole group should join in for the refrain. Practice using your voice and body gestures to dramatize the lines. Then, perform for the class.

THE GUPPY

by Ogden Nash
Adapted for choral reading by Mary Young Williams

Whales have calves,
Cats have kittens,
Bears have cubs,
Bats have bittens,
Swans have cygnets,
Seals have puppies,
But, guppies just have
little guppies.

ADAPTATION:

Narrator:	"The Guppy" by Ogden Nash
Reader 1:	Whales have calves,
All:	Guppies have little guppies.
Reader 2:	Cats have kittens,
All:	Guppies have little guppies.
Reader 1:	Bears have cubs,
All:	Guppies have little guppies.
Reader 2:	Bats have bittens,
All:	Guppies have little guppies.
Reader 3:	Swans have cygnets,
All:	Guppies have little guppies.
Reader 4:	Seals have puppies,
All:	But, guppies just have little guppies.

From *Verses From 1929 On* by Ogden Nash. Reprinted by permission of Little, Brown and Company.

MORE TO DO

CHORAL READING/SCIENCE
Following the pattern in the poem, name other animals and their babies. Work in a group to make a class presentation of your creation.

CHORAL READING/SOCIAL STUDIES
Use this pattern to prepare a script about states and their capitals.

All:	Madison
Reader 1:	Is Wisconsin's capital.
All:	Augusta
Reader 2:	Is the capital of Maine.
All:	And Austin
Reader 3:	Is the capital of Texas.
All:	How could I ever forget!

PROCEDURES: Look at the original poem so that you can get a sense of the poem and see how to adapt it into a choral reading. Use tape recordings and videotapes to help students dramatize the material.

Read this fable. Then prepare a script for doing a choral reading of it. Use the moral of the fable as a refrain throughout. The sample below will give you a start on your script. Finish it on your own.

THE FOX AND THE CROW

A Fable
Retold by Mary Young Williams

Clutching a morsel of cheese in her beak, the Crow flew high in a tree. A Fox spied the cheese and begged for a bite. The Crow shook her head to signify "No!" But this sly Fox had a plan. He turned his face up to the crow and cried, "Behold your magnificence! See how your ebony feathers are kissed by the sun. When I gaze upon you, my eyes perceive the most breathtaking glamour in all of nature!"

The Crow strutted proudly back and forth, tossing her beak with each word. The sly Fox went on softly, "And you're musical, too! The beauty of your voice is unsurpassed. If only I could hear you sing! Your songs would set my heart to dancing!"

The Crow, swept away by the Fox's flattery, opened her beak to sing. Of course, as soon as she did, the cheese dropped straight to the ground. The Fox snapped it up with a satisfied smile.

Humming smugly to himself, the Fox slipped into the forest. Before disappearing, he called back to the vain and sorry Crow, "Maybe the next time you'll know better . . . Don't trust flatterers!"

SAMPLE SCRIPT

Narrator:	"The Fox and the Crow," a fable.
Girls:	Clutching a morsel of cheese in her beak, a Crow flew high in a tree.
All:	DON'T TRUST FLATTERERS.
Boys:	A fox spied the cheese and begged for a bite.
All:	DON'T TRUST FLATTERERS.
Girls:	The Crow shook her head to signify "No!"
All:	DON'T TRUST FLATTERERS.
	(and so forth)

PROCEDURES: First, have students preread the fable silently and then read it aloud together before writing their individual scripts. Suggest that they develop the scripts so that all students can participate in the groups; for example, all boys, all girls, short students, tall students, and all students. Have small groups select some of the scripts to prepare for presentation.

Present a choral reading of this poem.

ARITHMETIC
by Carl Sandburg

Adapted for choral reading by Mary Young Williams
A = All (for the choral refrain and unison lines) *B = Boys* *G = Girls*

A: "Arithmetic," a poem by Carl Sandburg.

A: Arithmetic is where
B: numbers fly like pigeons
G: in and out of your head.

A: Arithmetic tells you
B: how many times you lose or win
G: if you know how many you had before you lost or won.

A: Arithmetic is
B: seven eleven all good children go to heaven
G: – or five six bundle of sticks.

A: Arithmetic is
B: numbers you squeeze from your head to your hand
G: to your pencil to your paper till you get the answer.

A: Arithmetic is
B: where the answer is right and everything is nice
G: and you look out the window and see the blue sky
B: – or the answer is wrong and you have to start all over
G: and try again and see how it comes out this time.

A: If you take a number
and double it and double it again
and then double it a few more times,
the number gets bigger and bigger
and goes higher and higher
and only arithmetic can tell you
what the number is
when you decide to quit doubling.

A: Arithmetic is
B: where you have to multiply–
G: and you carry the multiplication table in your head
B: and hope you won't lose it.

(continued on the next page)

A: If you have two animal crackers, one good and one bad, and you eat one and a striped zebra with streaks all over him eats the other how many animal crackers will you have if
somebody offers you
five, six, seven
G: and you say No no no
B: and you say Nay nay nay
A: and you say Nix nix nix?

A: If you ask your mother for one fried egg for breakfast
and she gives you two fried eggs
and you eat both of them,
who is better in arithmetic,
you or your mother?

MORE TO DO

WORD PROBLEMS/MATH
Work in small groups to brainstorm word problems, following the pattern in "Arithmetic": If you have two animal crackers, one good and one bad . . . Read your word problems aloud to the class. Teams can challenge each other to give the correct answers.

CHANTING
In small groups, brainstorm other chants and rhymes about numbers. For example:

> Five, ten, no money to spend.
> Fifteen, twenty, not even a penny.

MATH PROBLEM SKITS
Working in a small group, plan a skit that demonstrates addition and subtraction problems. Use props to dramatize the facts of the problems. Challenge the audience to give the correct answer.

READERS' THEATER
In groups of four, practice doing this choral reading script as a readers' theater script. Then perform it in front of the class.

PROCEDURES: Divide the class into two groups, arranging by voice tone. Practice getting voices and timing coordinated. Try doing the entire poem as a unison, refrain, or two-part reading.

First, try a unison choral reading of this poem, arranging yourselves by voice tones: light, medium, and dark. Then work with your group to rewrite the poem for choral refrain or two-part or multiple-part work. Perform your script for the class.

THE DONKEY
(Anonymous)

I saw a donkey
    One day old,
His head was too big
    For his neck to hold;
His legs were shaky
    and long and loose,
They rocked and staggered
    And weren't much use.
He tried to gambol
    And frisk a bit,
But he wasn't quite sure
    Of the trick of it.
His queer little coat
    Was soft and gray
And curled at his neck
    In a lovely way.
His face was wistful
    And left no doubt
That he felt life needed
    Some thinking about.
So he blundered round
    In venturesome quest,
And then lay flat
    On the ground to rest.
He looked so little
    And weak and slim,
I prayed the world
    Might be good to him.

PROCEDURES: You might want to tape the students' performance to play back to them. Be sure to model scriptwriting (see Guide Sheets 4 and 5, pages 43–44) before asking students to write their own scripts. You might suggest "hee-haw" to groups who want a choral refrain.

Readers' Theater

Definition: The reading of a script that already exists in play form or that has been developed from a story, text material, or a poem, with primary emphasis placed on how much drama the readers put into it.

Activity Sheets

In your group, practice four different ways of saying each of these expressions. Make them "come alive" by changing your tone of voice and by putting emotions into the words. Use body movements and change your facial expressions to go along with the words.

MY WORD!

1. Say "He's smart" as if to mean . . .
   a. he is *not* smart.
   b. he is very intelligent.
   c. he is a wise guy!.
   d. you are not sure if he is smart or not.
2. Say "I'm thirsty" as said by . . .
   a. the last person in line for the water fountain.
   b. the pitcher after a close game.
   c. a person who has been lost in the desert.
   d. an angry child.
3. Say "Ah" as said by . . .
   a. a grandparent looking at the first grandchild.
   b. a child picking up a worm.
   c. a person who banged a thumb with a hammer.
   d. a 10-year-old when realizing it's Saturday
4. Ask "What time is it?" as asked by . . .
   a. a 13-year-old taking a test.
   b. a person waking up.
   c. a parent waiting for a child to return home from a date.
   d. someone waiting for midnight on New Year's Eve.

MORE TO DO

BRAINSTORMING
Work in groups to brainstorm other expressions and decide different ways they could be said. Teams can challenge each other to guess what situations would cause the different tones of voice.

PROCEDURES: These are excellent warm-up activities for students to practice using their voices as instruments. Let them use a tape recorder and work in front of a mirror so they can better evaluate their voices, facial expressions, and body gestures. In class presentations, make suggestions for improvement.

Practice the readers' theater script of this poem in your groups. It has lots of opportunities for you to use props and dramatize with your voice, face, and body. Then perform it for the class.

HABITS OF THE HIPPOPOTAMUS
by Arthur Guiterman
Adapted for readers' theater by Mary Young Williams
6 readers: 3 girls and 3 boys

1 girl: "Habits of the Hippopotamus," a poem by Arthur Guiterman

3 girls: The hippopotamus is strong
And huge of head and broad of bustle;
3 boys: The limbs on which he rolls along
Are big with
All: hippopotamuscle.

3 girls: He does not greatly care for sweets
Like ice cream, apple pie or custard,
3 boys: But takes to flavor what he eats
A little
All: hippopotamustard.

3 girls: The hippopotamus is true
To all his principles, and just;
3 boys: He always tries his best to do
The things one
All: hippopotamust.

3 boys: He never rides in trucks or trams,
In taxicabs or omnibuses,
3 girls: And so keeps out of traffic jams
And other
All: hippopotamusses.

MORE TO DO

RESEARCH AND WRITING SCIENCE
Use encyclopedias and science books to find accurate information about the characteristics of the hippopotamus. Add more stanzas to this poem and present them to the class.

CHORAL READING
Work as a class to prepare a script of this poem for choral reading. Use all class members. Remember, you can set it up for choral refrain, two-part work, unison, or multiple-part work. Invite another class to come to your performance.

PROCEDURES: Help them develop interesting ways to dramatize the action using props. Use choral reading techniques with this.

Your group will rewrite this poem into a readers' theater script. Think of various ways to assign reading parts. Practice reading and dramatizing your script before presenting it to the class.

ELETELEPHONY
by Laura E. Richards

Once there was an elephant,
Who tried to use the telephant—

No! No! I mean an elephone
Who tried to use the telephone

(Dear me! I am not certain quite
That even now I've got it right.)

Howe'er it was, he got his trunk
Entangled in the telephunk;

The more he tried to get it free,
The louder buzzed the telephee—

(I fear I'd better drop the song
Of elephop and telephong!)

From *Tirra Lirra, Rhymes Old and New* by Laura E. Richards
(Boston: Little, Brown & Company, 1932).

MORE TO DO

GROUP DISCUSSION AND WRITING/SCIENCE
Talk about other inventions and write some nonsense poems about them. Perform some as readers' theater scripts.

PROCEDURES: Review with students the sample script for poetry on Guide Sheet 5, page 44. Groups might write two or three versions to see which one they like best. Try to get a good variety for the class presentations. Let the class discuss how well each presentation put drama into the script.

Work in your groups and practice ways to say the lines and to dramatize this readers' theater script with facial expressions and body language. Use props and costumes if you want. Prepare a presentation.

PAUL REVERE'S RIDE
by Henry Wadsworth Longfellow
A short version, adapted for readers' theater by Mary Young Williams for 5 readers.

Reader 5:	"Paul Revere's Ride," a poem by Henry Wadsworth Longfellow
Reader1:	Listen, my children, and you shall hear Of the midnight ride of Paul Revere.
Reader 2:	On the eighteenth of April, in Seventy-five; Hardly a man is now alive
Reader 3:	Who remembers that famous day and year,
Reader 5:	*(deep voice)* The midnight ride of Paul Revere.
Reader 4:	He said to his friend, "If the British march By land or sea from the town tonight,
Reader 2:	Hang a lantern aloft in the belfry arch Of the North Church tower as a signal light—
Reader 1:	One, if by land, and two, if by sea; And I on the opposite shore will be,
Reader 3:	Ready to ride and spread the alarm Through every Middlesex village and farm, For the country folk to be up and to arm.
Reader 5:	*(deep voice)* The midnight ride of Paul Revere.
Reader 1:	Booted and spurred, with a heavy stride On the opposite shore walked Paul Revere Now he patted his horse's side Now gazed at the landscape far and near,
Reader 2:	Then, impetuous, stamped the earth, And turned and tightened his saddle-girth;
Reader 3:	But mostly he watched with eager search The belfry-tower of the Old North Church,
Reader 4:	As it rose above the graves on the hill, Lonely and spectral and somber and still.
Reader 1:	And lo! as he looks, on the belfry's height A glimmer, and then a gleam of light!
Reader 2:	He springs to the saddle, the bridle he turns, But lingers and gazes, till full on his sight
Reader 3:	A second lamp in the belfry burns!

(continued on the next page)

Reader 5:	*(deep voice)* The midnight ride of Paul Revere.
Reader 4:	The hurry of hoofs in a village street, A shape in the moonlight, a bulk in the dark,
Reader 2:	And beneath from the pebbles, in passing, a spark Struck bout by a steed flying fearless and fleet—
Reader 1:	That was all! And yet through the gloom and light, The fate of the nation was riding that night;
Reader 3:	The spark struck out by that steed, in his flight, Kindled the land into flame with its heat,
Reader 5:	*(deep voice)* The midnight ride of Paul Revere.
Reader 1:	So through the night rode Paul Revere; And so through the night went his cry of alarm To every Middlesex village and farm—
Reader 2:	A cry of defiance and not of fear,
Reader 3:	A voice in the darkness, a knock at the door!
Reader 4:	And a word that shall echo forevermore!
Reader 5:	The midnight ride of Paul Revere.
Reader 1:	For, borne on the night-wind of the Past, Through all our history, to the last,
Reader 2:	In the hour of darkness and peril and need,
Reader 3:	The people will waken and listen to hear
Reader 4:	The hurrying hoof-beats of that steed,
Reader 5:	And the midnight message of Paul Revere.
All:	THE BRITISH ARE COMING!

Adapted from "Paul Revere's Ride" in *Children's Own Longfellow* by Henry Wadsworth Longfellow (Boston: Houghton Mifflin Company, 1908).

MORE TO DO

GROUP DISCUSSION/ SOCIAL STUDIES

Review the events that surrounded Paul Revere's midnight ride and talk about its importance to the American Revolution. Then form groups to discuss the struggle for freedom in the colonies. Give your own personal definition of freedom and tell what you would do to keep yours.

IMPROVISATION/SOCIAL STUDIES

Form groups to plan improvisations of Paul Revere's ride. Write dialogue in the dialect of the day. Mention geographical locations (Lexington, Concord) and historical figures (William Dawes, Samuel Prescott).

PROCEDURES: Let each group of five assign the speaking parts to its members. Encourage the use of props and costumes. Invite another class in to watch. Relate the poem to the universal human struggle for freedom.

This readers' theater script presents a traditional folktale. Assign speaking parts to members of your group. Practice the script before presenting it to the class.

THE THREE WISHES
A Folktale
Retold and adapted for readers' theater by Mary Young Williams
for four readers: Readers 1 and 2, Man, and Woman.

Reader 1:	"The Three Wishes," a folktale.
Reader 2:	Long ago in a little house in the woods lived a man and a woman who had very little to eat. The man cut firewood for a living, but he did not make much money at it.
Man:	Though I work very hard, we never seem to have enough; my wife and I are very hungry.
Reader 1:	After he said those words, a little fairy peeked at him from the grass at his feet and startled him.
Reader 2:	Looking at the man with sympathetic eyes, the fairy granted the man three wishes.
Man:	Three wishes! Three wishes! The first three things I wish for, I will get! I can't believe my good fortune today!
Reader 1:	Then, the fairy vanished, and the man hurried home to tell his wife the good news.
Man:	Dear woman, come here! I have such good news!
Woman:	Why are you so excited?
Reader 2:	The woman raced to her husband, and he told her about the fairy and the three wishes. The woman gasped!
Woman:	You mean we can wish for anything, and it will be ours?
Man:	Yes! The fairy promised that we will get our first three wishes!
Reader 1:	The man and woman sat at their table, gabbing about their wishes. Being hungry, they nibbled bread while they talked.
Man:	Just think, dear woman, we can ask for anything!
Woman:	Yes, I envision a big, big house.
Man:	I dream about us as King and Queen.
Woman:	I have always wanted children! We could have five boys and five girls.
Man:	I like boys best! We will have *six* boys and four girls.

(continued on the next page)

Woman: Just think about it! All the money we ever wanted awaits us!

Reader 2: They talked into the evening about all the things they had ever dreamed of. They plotted to use their three wishes wisely. Soon the bread on the table was gone, and the man noticed his hunger.

Man: I wish we had a big sausage on the table!

Woman: Oh, no! Look! You have wasted one of our wishes for a sausage! Only two wishes remain for us now.

Man: I'm so sorry! In my hunger, I did not think. I forgot and wished for something to eat. Stay happy, though. We have two wishes left. Just think, dear woman, we can still wish for anything!

Woman: Yes, thoughts of a mansion dance in my head.

Man: Thinking of being King and Queen excites me!

Woman: Just think! Money would pile high at our feet!

Reader 1: In the meantime, the wasted wish kept grating on the woman's nerves. She nagged her husband about that first miserable wish for the sausage.

Woman: Oh, how could you have wished for that old, nasty sausage! Didn't you think before you made the wish? Look at that old sausage! How I hate to see that old sausage on the table!

Reader 2: The woman's piercing voice and insulting words jabbed her husband.

Man: Why can't you forget about the sausage? You talk too much! Sausage, sausage, sausage! Stop talking about the sausage! I wish that sausage were at the end of your nose!

Reader 1: All of a sudden, a sausage popped out on the end of the woman's nose.

Woman: EEEEEE! Husband, what have you done!

Reader 2: Not knowing what to do about the sausage at the end of his wife's nose, the man tried to pull it free, but no luck! After many jerks and yanks, he stopped trying.

Man: One wish! We have one more wish left. Enough money to buy anything we want is still in our grasp.

Woman: Who cares? When people see this sausage on my nose, they'll laugh!

(continued on the next page)

Man: A Queen! I'll wish for you to be my Queen.

Woman: Who cares, Husband? When people see this sausage on my nose, they'll laugh!

Reader 1: Depressed, the man sighed heavily about his wife's nose and the sausage dangling from its tip.

Man: I really wish you did not have that sausage at the end of your nose!

Reader 2: With his words, the sausage disappeared at once. In a instant, the couple's dreams vanished. Their wishes of money, children, a big house, and being King and Queen dissolved.

Reader 1: Now the sausage was gone from the woman's nose, and there was no bread left in the house, so the man trudged off into the woods to cut firewood. He chopped enough to put bread on the table again, but thoughts of the three wishes and all their lost riches haunted him for the rest of his days.

MORE TO DO

IMPROVISATION
Work in pairs to improvise skits for this tale. Some of the dialogue between the man and woman is already there for you to memorize, but you will have to create more by changing the narration. Add pantomime. Practice and perform for the class.

STORYTELLING
Visualize the sequence of events in the story. Take notes of key words and phrases that will help you remember the events. Give a storytelling presentation to a class of primary students.

ROUND TABLE DISCUSSION
Join a round table group to discuss having three wishes to solve your problems. Focus on key words such as *greed, comfort, wisdom,* and *misfortune*. Select one member to tell your classmates the results of your discussion.

PROCEDURES: Divide the class into four "stage" areas to practice the readers' theater scripts. Emphasize using voice intonation, eye contact, and body posture to dramatize the reading. Have the class evaluate the performances. Try the same script for choral reading, pantomime, puppet play, or story theater.

Read this tale and create a readers' theater script for it. (To get started, see the sample script at the end of the story.) Share your script with your group, and select one script to present to an audience.

UNCLE TOAD AND THE KING OF HEAVEN
A Vietnamese Folktale
Retold by Mary Young Williams

A toad's barely audible croak chiseled into the motionless air of Vietnam. The dry lily pad crackled under his flaky body. Knowing that the little moisture still left in the mud would be gone in the near future, the toad gathered up his failing strength and croaked, "We need rain! Every creature on earth has fallen victim to the merciless rays of the sun. I must travel to the King of Heaven and beg for his help!"

Toad hopped off the lily pad and leaped across the dry, cracked rice fields. As he struggled through the parched countryside, Toad noticed a swarm of buzzing bees hovering around the dried petals of nectarless flowers. The bees buzzed a question to Toad: "Why do you travel afar? Surely your mud offers more moisture than this dusty road!"

"I'm traveling to the Heavens to find the King," croaked Toad. "I intend to complain to him about the Rain God's negligence." At that news, the bees begged to join him.

After traveling a few miles, Toad and the Bees came upon a very dehydrated Tiger who whimpered at the mere effort of raising his head. The travelers felt compassion and invited him to join them on their pilgrimage. The Tiger, his eyes filled with new resolve, raised himself slowly from the cracked, brown earth and set off with Toad and the Bees.

The weary travelers endured the heat of the journey for many days. One morning, they found a lonely Rooster clawing at the dust. Startled by visitors, the Rooster wept openly and confided his woes. "The new chicks are all dead and buried, and all the grain is gone. How can the Heavens be so merciless?" Rooster hung his head low and waved a weak wing at the cracked field.

The Tiger roared, "Come with us! We're going to visit the King of Heaven to plead for all earth's creatures." Rooster ruffled his feathers as though he felt a new surge of life in his thin body, then gratefully trudged off with the others.

They traveled many days, with Toad and Rooster riding on Tiger's back and the Bees buzzing along ahead. At last they left the parched earth behind and leaped from cloud to cloud, up to the Gates of Heaven. Here they huddled together to plan how they would present their complaint to the King.

(continued on the next page)

Finally Toad croaked, "I am ready to face the King. When I call, you must come immediately." Toad then leaped majestically across the hall and landed at the King's feet. He looked up and croaked, "Your Majesty, Your Majesty . . . "

Taken aback by the intrusion of this small and ugly toad, the King waved his arms and summoned the guards to remove the creature. Seeing the guards approaching, Toad quickly croaked, "Bees, help! Bees, help!"

The Bees came swarming around the guards, stinging viciously until the guards pleaded for mercy and dashed from the hall. Toad spoke up once again, "Your Majesty, Your Majesty . . ."

Heedless of the urgency in Toad's voice, the angry King boomed, "Vicious Dogs, Vicious Dogs, attack this intruder!" Growling, the dogs rushed into the hall.

Toad quickly sputtered, "Tiger! Tiger! Rush to my side!" The Tiger charged into the hall and embraced the Vicious Dogs in his powerful forelegs. They clawed, nipped, and howled at each other, their vicious dance tearing up the King's hall. It came to an abrupt halt when the Tiger took one ferocious swipe at the dogs' heads. The dogs, fearing for their lives, limped and yelped out the door.

Once again, Toad pleaded, "Your Majesty, Your Majesty . . ."

Abruptly, the King summoned the Thunder and Lightning God. With his enormous mallet, the Thunder and Lightning God pounded the rhythm of his anger. He charged at the Toad, but Toad croaked loudly, "Rooster, help! Rooster, help!"

Rooster flapped into the hall. With wings waving, claws scratching, and beak slashing, Rooster dove at the Thunder and Lightning God. Now, there is nothing the Thunder and Lightning God fears—nothing, that is, except roosters. At the sight of this shrieking bird, the Thunder and Lightning God covered his head and dashed from the hall.

Dismayed by the disorder of his court, the King of Heaven shouted, "Uncle Toad, please stop your attack. I will listen to you."

Toad sat up very tall, pleased and proud that the King had called him Uncle, since the word "Uncle" symbolizes respect and affection in Vietnam. Hopping up to the throne, Toad cleared his throat and began, "Your Majesty, the Rain God deserted earth and left us with a devastating drought. All living creatures are dying. We traveled here to plead with you to send rain to earth."

(continued on the next page)

The King bowed to Uncle Toad and promised, "Of course! I will speak to the Rain God about this immediately." Then, looking in dismay at the disorder of his court, the King continued, "Uncle Toad, next time the earth needs rain, please save yourself a trip. Do not come all the way to my Kingdom. Just croak, and I will make sure the Rain God sprinkles the earth with rain."

Toad agreed to this arrangement. Even today, when you hear a croaking toad, he is telling the Heavens that the earth needs rain.

SAMPLE SCRIPT

To create a script, list the characters and decide how many readers you want to narrate the story. This sample is just one way you might start.

Reader 1: "Uncle Toad and the King of Heaven," a Vietnamese folktale.

Reader 2: A toad's barely audible croak chiseled into the motionless air of Vietnam. The dry lily pad crackled under his flaky body.

Reader 3: Knowing that the little moisture still left in the mud would be gone in the near future, the toad gathered up his failing strength and croaked.

Toad: We need rain! Every creature on earth has fallen victim to the merciless rays of the sun. I must travel to the King of Heaven and beg for his help!

Reader 1: (echoing) I must travel to the King of Heaven and beg for his help!

MORE TO DO

STORYTELLING
Maybe your group can visit some primary classrooms to tell this tale. Prepare ahead by making notes about the sequence of events and rehearsing.

BUZZ GROUPS
Work in buzz groups to list other possible reasons why toads croak. Create other tales like this one, using the theme of respect for the creatures of nature.

PROCEDURES: Tell the students that if they like, they can create original dialogue for their script, having the characters talk more to each other. Look at the script for "The Three Wishes" for further guidance. Have students work alone to prepare scripts before they work in groups. Have each group make a readers' theater presentation.

Storytelling

Definition: A way of sharing stories that goes beyond the simple retelling of them by using voice, facial expressions, and body language to make the word "images come alive with emotion.

Activity Sheets

Read this fable to yourself. Then block out your own version of the story, listing the events in sequence. Tell the story in a dramatic way to a small group. Choose one group member to tell it to the class.

THE WOLF IN SHEEP'S CLOTHING
A Fable
Retold by Mary Young Williams

For months, the lurking, hungry Wolf pondered how he might grab himself a plump sheep from the shepherd's fold. Fortune fell upon him when he found a sheep's skin and devised his grand scheme.

"What great luck! If I wear this sheep's skin, the sheep will think I'm one of the fold!" Joyfully, Wolf slipped into the woolly skin and moved, unnoticed, among the sheep. Whenever he was hungry, the Wolf in disguise feasted on a plump sheep.

The puzzled shepherd wondered about his dwindling flock. Each night he kept guard, alert for a wolf who was attacking the fold. Finding nothing, he would return to his tent and sleep restlessly.

One night, the shepherd's craving for mutton was strong, and he grabbed an animal from the fold for his evening meal. Thinking it was one of his sheep, the shepherd killed the wolf in sheep's clothing.

When he realized that he had destroyed the wolf who had been devouring his sheep, the shepherd rejoiced. He looked at the dead wolf and observed, "Those who bring harm to others often bring harm to themselves."

BLOCKING OUT THE STORY

TITLE: A Wolf in Sheep's Clothing

FIRST SENTENCE: A hungry wolf found a sheep's skin and hatched a grand plot.

STORY SEQUENCE: (List events that move the story along.)

- When the Wolf slipped into the sheep's skin, he found he could move easily among the sheep.
-
-
-
-

LAST SENTENCE: The moral is, those who bring harm to others often bring harm to themselves.

PROCEDURES: You may want to use an overhead transparency to complete the sequence of events with the whole class. Work with other fables too, until students get used to blocking out the stories. Explain that you will require them to do this for every storytelling activity. Then have the class form small groups to practice their storytelling skills.

Read this tall tale to yourself. Then have one member of your group read it aloud. Block out the story by listing key phrases that indicate the sequence of events. Tell your own version of the tale. Use voice, facial expression, and body gestures to make it come alive.

HOW PAUL BUNYAN DUG THE COLUMBIA RIVER
A Tall Tale

There's many conflictin' stories about how Paul dug the Columbia River, but of course, there's only one right one and that's the one I was just tellin' about the Inland Empire. I was right there and I saw how it was done. When Paul got his raft of logs finished and was ready to take 'em out, he just went out there and plowed out the river. And there wasn't nothin' to it at all. He plowed it out first and then filled it up with the water and evened it out so it would be nice and smooth for his logs to slide over. On a windy day in the Gorge when an east wind is blowin', you can see the hole yet in the water where Paul never put in the last bucketful when he was evenin' it out.

MORE TO DO

BRAINSTORMING AND STORYTELLING/SOCIAL STUDIES
Working in a small group, select a major river or mountain range in the United States and prepare tall tales about it. Brainstorm facts you know about your choice and the geographical area it is in. Tell each other tall tales that combine these facts with exaggeration.

STORYTELLING/SCIENCE
As a review for a test, tell a tall tale about a scientific discovery that combines facts from textbooks and encyclopedias with exaggeration.

IMPROVISATION
Read other tales about Paul Bunyan and Babe, the Blue Ox. Then work in groups to perform improvisational skits based on them.

PROCEDURES: Be sure students know about Paul Bunyan, the legendary hero of the lumber camps of the American Northwest. Have them write the sequence of events before telling their stories. Encourage them to read other tall tales and tell them in their groups.

Read this pourquoi tale from Africa. "Pourquoi" is the French word for "why," so a "pourquoi tale" tells why something happened. Prepare yourself to tell the story to your classmates. Practice using your voice, face, and body to make the storytelling dramatic.

WHY THE SUN AND MOON ARE IN THE SKY
An African Folktale
Retold by Mary Young Williams

A long time ago, the Sun and Moon lived happily together on the earth. They enjoyed talking with their friend, Water. The Sun and Moon loved to entertain friends, so they invited Water to visit them.

Though very excited about the invitation, Water declined, stating that he and his family did not go out to visit very often. Suspecting that he was being shy, Sun and Moon insisted. Once again, Water declined and finally told them of his embarrassment over the size of his large family. Water told the Sun and Moon that he appreciated their kindness, but it would be wiser if he did not come.

Again Sun and Moon pleaded, "We are your friends. Our home is more than big enough for you! Please do not hesitate to come!" Water swished with pleasure upon hearing this testimony of their friendship and finally accepted their persistent invitation.

Water and all his family splashed joyfully to visit Sun and Moon, who soon realized that their home was being swallowed up. Sun and Moon rose to get above the Water as first the floor, then the roof disappeared under its wet presence. Finally Sun and Moon kissed their friend good-by, telling Water he could remain there with his large family and they would find a home elsewhere.

Sun and Moon rose to the Sky and and gazed down upon their former home. They thought about Water's warnings. Indeed, Water had been sensitive to worry about the amount of room he and his family needed. Smiling, Sun and Moon shone down on Water with happiness, because they knew that their kindness had touched his heart deeply. Even today, from their home in the Sky, Sun and Moon look down fondly on the earth, glowing brightly and spreading rays of happiness over all.

MORE TO DO

GROUP DISCUSSION AND STORYTELLING/SCIENCE

Work in groups to compare this tale to the scientific facts. Then use facts about the solar system to make up a pourquoi tale of your own. Tell the tale to your classmates.

PROCEDURES: Have small groups of students try the round robin storytelling method. "Round robin" means one person starts telling the story and then stops; the next person continues the story from that point, and so on. Divide the story into enough parts so that each group member has one part to tell.

Here is the beginning of the story of Chicken Little. It is a cumulative tale, which means that part of the story repeats itself over and over, each time a new character is added. Follow the directions and use the characters listed below to keep the tale going in your group.

CHICKEN LITTLE
A Cumulative Tale

One day Chicken Little was eating corn in the barnyard when—whack! Something hit her on the head. "Goodness gracious me!" said Chicken Little, "The sky's a-going to fall! I must go and tell the king."

So she went along, and she went along, and she went along, till she met Henny Penny. "Where are you going, Chicken Little?" asked Henny Penny.

"Oh, I'm going to tell the king that the sky's a-fallin'," said Chicken Little.

"May I come with you?" asked Henny Penny.

"Certainly," said Chicken Little. So, Chicken Little and Henny Penny went to tell the king that the sky was falling.

SAMPLE PATTERN

1. Continue the story, repeating from the second paragraph and adding these new characters: Cocky Locky, Ducky Lucky, Goosey Loosey, Turkey Lurkey, Foxy Loxy. Each time, repeat this line:
   So, they went along, and they went along, and they went along till they met — — (character).
2. When you have all seven characters, start winding down.
   Soon, however, Foxy Loxy went into his cave. He didn't go very far, but turned around to wait for Chicken Little, Henny Penny, Cocky Locky, Ducky Lucky, Goosey Loosey, and Turkey Lurkey to follow him.
3. Now follow the pattern below, repeating from "So at last."
   So at last, (character) went through the dark hole into the cave. (Character) hadn't gone very far when "Hrumph!" Foxy Loxy snapped off (his/her) head, and threw the body over his left shoulder.
4. Learn these lines to end the story.
   But Foxy Loxy had to make two bites at Henny Penny. When the first snap only hurt Henny Penny and didn't kill her, she had time to call out. Chicken Little turned tail and off she ran home; so she never got to tell the king the sky was falling.

MORE TO DO
GROUP DISCUSSION
Discuss with your classmates Chicken Little's ability to convince the others that "the sky's a-fallin'." Compare this with the propaganda techniques used by politicians. Discuss how hysteria might have been prevented. How does this apply to real life?

PROCEDURES: Once students have mastered the telling of this cumulative tale, they can try others, using the pattern on this page to block their stories.

Read this summary of a classic fairy tale. Practice telling the story in your group, using the familiar lines listed after the story, and adding your own touches. Then tell the story to your classmates. Use voice, face, and body expressions to show emotions and to add drama.

SNOW WHITE
A Fairy Tale
Retold by Mary Young Williams

The princess Snow White lives in a castle with her stepmother, the Queen. The vain Queen despises Snow White because she is so beautiful. For years, the Queen's magic mirror has told her that she is the fairest woman in the land. But one day, the mirror whispers to the Queen that Snow White is the most beautiful. The furious Queen orders a huntsman to take Snow White to the woods, kill her, and cut out her heart.

The huntsman, overcome by Snow White's generous and kind heart, cannot kill her. Instead, he returns to the castle with the heart of a boar and lies to the Queen. Snow White roams through the forest in search of a home, until she discovers the home of seven dwarfs, who invite her to stay with them.

When the Queen cradles her magic mirror and once again hears that Snow White is the fairest in the land, she knows that the huntsman lied. Disguising herself as a poor old woman, the Queen sets out to destroy the girl herself.

At the house of the seven dwarfs, she finds Snow White alone and tempts her to bite into a poisoned apple. The apple catches in Snow White's throat, and she falls dead. The seven dwarfs grieve her loss. They place her in a glass casket so they can gaze upon her beauty forever.

After a long, long time, a handsome Prince arrives. When he sees Snow White, he falls to his knees and kisses her. The kiss forces the poison apple out of her throat and Snow White comes to life. The prince and Snow White ride off to his palace, and together they make plans for a royal wedding. Upon hearing this news from the mirror, the Queen smashes her mirror into pieces and dies instantly.

FAMILIAR LINES

Magic mirror on the wall,
Who is the fairest of us all?

Thou art the fairest, Lady Queen.

Oh, Lady Queen, thou still art fair,
But none to Snow White can compare.

Deep within the forest glen,
She lives with seven little men.

PROCEDURES: Have copies of the Snow White story available for students to refer to as they prepare for this storytelling. Students can follow the suggestions on Guide Sheet 10, page 49, to block their stories on note cards. Divide students into small groups to practice. After the presentations, discuss the performances.

Spin-Offs

Choral Reading

- Students can prepare a holiday package of scripts for choral reading. Follow these suggestions:
  1. Focus on a theme for the holidays.
  2. Find a variety of materials—poems, stories, song lyrics, personal writings.
  3. Have five groups each write a script from the materials.
  4. Present a choral reading medley production.
  5. Travel to other classes to share the holiday message.
- Use Guide Sheet 5, page 44, to help students turn poetry into scripts for group choral readings. Use the first few minutes of class time for several days to let the groups present their choral readings. Follow these suggestions:
  1. Have five small groups select five poems to turn into scripts.
  2. Provide time for the groups to rehearse.
  3. Set up a master calendar so that one script can be presented a day. Think about it: five groups present five scripts each, providing twenty-five moments of enjoyment for your classes.What a pleasant way to begin an instructional day!
  4. Prior to the day of the group's performance, schedule five minutes of rehearsal time for them, either before lunch or during recess.
- Videotape some of the choral reading presentations. Have students watch the tapes and make suggestions for improving their body gestures, facial expressions, and voice quality.
- Have students rewrite Mother Goose rhymes into script form for choral reading and perform them in the primary classrooms so that the younger children can interact with the materials. Students might also work with stories such as Kipling's *Just So Stories* to prepare and present choral reading scripts to other classes.

Readers' Theater

- Tell students to offer their scriptwriting services to other teachers. (Beforehand, make arrangements with teachers who are interested and prepare a list of those teachers for the students.) Have students work with the text materials currently being covered by the teachers, rewriting them into script form. Then they can perform the readers' theater pieces for the different classes.

- Let a group of student volunteers act as tutors in classrooms with teachers who want to try the readers' theater technique. Instruct the students to help the other classes with scriptwriting as well as the performances.
- Students could prepare favorite song lyrics as readers' theater presentations. Insist that the presentations not sound like songs but like scripts. Evaluate their interpretations.

Storytelling

- Have students work in groups to list modern-day heroes and heroines, such as music, movie, TV, and sports stars. Work with them as a whole class to select one hero or heroine and to list, in sequence, details in the story of that star's rise to fame. After modeling this technique, have students do the same thing in their groups for other stars. Then they should select one of their group members to tell the star's story to the class.
- Plan a Storytelling Hour once a week. For each session, schedule five of the school's outstanding storytellers. Let them select their own audience. Work with other teachers to coordinate this school-wide effort. For example, each teacher might nominate one storyteller from his or her class.
- Set up a Storytelling Troupe. Have the student storytellers visit different classrooms to tell stories. Organize this with other teachers.
- Teams can compete by challenging each other to "tell a tale." Have them pick a theme for a pourquoi tale, for example, why rose bushes have thorns. Allow each team two minutes to work out a story and select one spokesperson to tell it. Members of the other teams listen for a beginning, middle, and end in each story. Only if its story has all three does the team score a point.
- After students have created their pourquoi stories, form a panel with one representative from each group. The panel should debate the credibility of the stories and have the class vote to select the most convincing one.

Your name ______________________________ Date ______________

P = Poor
A = Average
C = Clever
E = Exceptional

RATE YOURSELF
Find your oral interpretation PACE rating.

GROUP WORK: You . . .	P	A	C	E
cooperated with everyone.				
followed and offered suggestions.				
followed directions.				
took part in planning.				
performed when called upon.				
gave others their turns to perform.				
didn't upstage others.				
helped others with problems.				

GETTING READY: You . . .	P	A	C	E
selected good readings.				
wrote realistic scripts.				
made good notes for storytelling.				
took part in casting performances.				
learned speaking parts.				
worked hard on character roles.				
practiced.				

PERFORMING: You . . .	P	A	C	E
followed the script or story.				
communicated roles by performing realistically.				
pronounced well and paused for good phrasing.				
projected well, adjusting volume and rate as needed.				
used body gestures that fit.				
fit facial expressions to emotions.				
fit voice pitch, intonation, and rhythm to roles.				
used dialects when needed.				
kept good eye contact with the audience.				
handled props and costumes well.				

Comment on what you did best in oral interpretation.

Comment on what was hardest for you.

What changes would you make the next time?

Classmate's name ________________________ Date __________

RATE A CLASSMATE
Find the oral interpretation PACE rating for a classmate in your group.

P = Poor
A = Average
C = Clever
E = Exceptional

GROUP WORK: This classmate . . .	P	A	C	E
cooperated with everyone.				
followed and offered suggestions.				
followed directions.				
took part in planning.				
performed when called upon.				
gave others their turns to perform.				
didn't upstage others.				
helped others with problems.				

GETTING READY: This classmate . . .	P	A	C	E
selected good readings.				
wrote realistic scripts.				
made good notes for storytelling.				
took part in casting performances.				
learned speaking parts.				
worked hard on character roles.				
practiced.				

PERFORMING: This classmate . . .	P	A	C	E
followed the script or story.				
communicated roles by performing realistically.				
pronounced well and paused for good phrasing.				
projected well, adjusting volume and rate as needed.				
used body gestures that fit.				
fit facial expressions to emotions.				
fit voice pitch, intonation, and rhythm to roles.				
used dialects when needed.				
kept good eye contact with the audience.				
handled props and costumes well.				

Comment on what your classmate did best in oral interpretation.

Comment on what seemed hardest for your classmate.

What changes would you suggest the next time?

Your name ________________________

Names of Group Members

Date ____________

______________________ ______________________
______________________ ______________________
______________________ ______________________

P = Poor
A = Average
C = Clever
E = Exceptional

RATE YOUR GROUP
Find your oral interpretation PACE rating.

GROUP WORK: The group members. . .

cooperated with everyone.				
followed and offered suggestions.				
followed directions.				
took part in planning.				
performed when called upon.				
gave others their turns to perform.				
didn't upstage others.				
helped others with problems.				

GETTING READY: The group members . . .

selected good readings.				
wrote realistic scripts.				
made good notes for storytelling.				
took part in casting performances.				
learned speaking parts.				
worked hard on character roles.				
practiced.				

PERFORMING: The group members . . .

followed the script or story.				
communicated roles by performing realistically.				
pronounced well and paused for good phrasing.				
projected well, adjusting volume and rate as needed.				
used body gestures that fit.				
fit facial expressions to emotions.				
fit voice pitch, intonation, and rhythm to roles.				
used dialects when needed.				
kept good eye contact with the audience.				
handled props and costumes well.				

Comment on what your group did best in oral interpretation.

Comment on what was hardest for your group.

What changes would you make the next time?

Your name ______________________

Group Discussion

I know that you believe
that you understand
what you think I said,
but I am not sure you realize
that what you heard
is not what I meant.

Getting Started in Group Discussion

"E-E-E-E-Ech, put them into groups!? What about control? How do I know they're really talking about the assignment? What about the freeloader? How do I manage the noise? They'll think it's party time!"

Yes, I wondered the same things and hid behind the wall of teacher-directed lessons. Then, I chanced it! I bruised slightly before learning a few *survival tips* about groups:

1. Never give them enough time—make them beg for more!
   If they have too much time, discipline problems result!
2. Give very clear, short jobs. Prepare by using this guide:
   "Within ___ minutes, your group will (name job).
   For example:
   "Within 5 minutes, your group leader will tell us the twenty ideas."
   "Within 10 minutes, your group will list five original topics."
3. Try to give each group member an assigned role.

More detailed help with group management appears on the guide sheets in this section.

Beware the muted, ditto-dominated classrooms where sound, an alien from the playyard, stays trapped within each silent body. Such classrooms deny students the enormous benefits of interaction. Small group discussions, while stimulating critical thinking, social skills, and processing skills, help shift student thinking into gear, and out of "neutral" or "park."

Your role as facilitator and moderator ensures that the groups run efficiently and effectively. While letting students talk among themselves in groups, you are always there to offer help in decision making, problem solving, and troubleshooting. Once you get over the initial panic of putting students into groups, and once you master the techniques for making it work, you will marvel at the efficiency of using groups to help students digest and articulate content material.

Think of yourself in your adult life. Don't you welcome a chance to brainstorm an idea with several people, just to hear new suggestions? Don't you seek other adults who share a common problem so that you can hear different perspectives? Don't all of us go into an interview situation wishing we had had more practice? If you acknowlege the need for group discussions in our adult lives, you will also recognize the value of giving students practice discussion time in our classes in all content areas.

I was facilitating groups in my classroom long before the recent flurry of interest in cooperative learning. I guarantee you that it works. Your students *do* learn in a spirit of cooperation when you set the standards for their small group discussions. Students learn to need and to respect their peers as they talk with each other.

The activities in this section offer group-discussion practice in several different forms: **interviewing, buzz groups, brainstorming, round table discussions, panel discussions,** and **role-play analysis.** See Guide Sheet 1, page 88, for descriptions of these forms.

Goals of Group Discussion

Social Goals

The student will

- learn the social skills needed for group work.
- practice cooperative interaction.
- develop poise and composure.
- build self-esteem.
- value the opinions of others.

Critical Thinking Goals

The student will

- make decisions.
- listen critically and purposefully.
- analyze and solve problems.
- use organizing, summarizing, and evaluating skills.
- identify and use concepts in discussion.

Group Discussion Goals

The student will

- increase vocabulary and ability to use language.
- learn and use group task roles.
- be articulate when speaking.
- keep to the discussion topic.
- give others their fair share of time to speak.
- support opinions.
- listen to different points of view.

Group Discussion Formats

Interviewing	Individuals ask questions of an interviewee to solicit information. Interviewer inquires, listens, gathers information, and condenses it.
Buzz Group	Members of small groups of five or six have a limited time to discuss and suggest solutions to a problem. The primary purpose is to acquaint group members with the problem and get them to generate questions about it.
Brainstorming	Members of small or large groups make suggestions about specific problems. The emphasis is on quantity of suggestions, and no ideas are rejected. Group members can add to, combine, or improve on the ideas of others.
Round Table Discussion	A small group of three to eight members and a moderator share ideas and deal with problems in an informal manner. The moderator guides the discussion, keeps the participants on topic, and summarizes and evaluates the results.
Panel Discussion	This is similar to round table, but more formal, with three to twelve group members. Each panel member acts as an authority on the topic. The audience is allowed to participate when the panel discussion is finished.
Role-Play Analysis	Large groups or the class as a whole discuss the outcomes presented in role-play enactments as a way of understanding various points of view. The role-play situations should progress from simple to more complex.

Guidelines for Interviews

1. Prepare for the interview. Know how to pronounce the person's name and find out what you should already know about that person.
2. Plan questions. Leave enough room on your question sheet for the answers.
3. Start with general questions. Ask about background and experience. Avoid yes-or-no questions.
4. Build on previous questions. Be ready to leave your prepared list briefly. Encourage the interviewee to give more details.
5. Practice being a good listener.
   - If interviewee is too general, ask for specific examples.
   - If there are too many details, ask what ties it together.
   - Repeat what the person has said to make sure you have it right.
   - Listen carefully to pick up hints of other things you could ask the person about.
   - Steer away from talk that has nothing to do with the topic.
6. Take simple notes.
   - Ask for the correct spelling of important key names and words.
   - If you quote the person exactly, ask the person to check it.
   - Keep the conversation going. Don't let your notetaking "slow down" the interview.
7. Be courteous.
   - An interview should be a polite conversation.
   - If you use a tape recorder, ask permission.
   - Speak clearly.
   - Follow up with a thank-you note.

The Effective Group Discussion Leader

Here are some guidelines for leading a discussion. Think also about the list of characteristics that help make a group discussion leader effective.

An Effective Group Discussion Leader . . .

1. Starts with an agenda/plans ahead.
2. Uses procedures that are understood by all group members.
3. Initiates the discussion.
4. Moves the discussion along.

An Effective Group Leader is . . .

Organized	Sets agendas, schedules time and place of meetings; notifies members; oversees tasks; keeps order; supplies materials.
Humble	Talks and acts naturally; facilitates but does not dominate.
Sensitive	Is firm but not defensive; is aware of interpersonal interactions; provides opportunities for everyone to express opinions; maintains a supportive climate.
Experienced	Grows into the role by learning about it and coming to understand and accept its responsibilities.
Attentive	Follows the discussion closely and summarizes it; keeps the group focused on tasks.

Roles in Group Discussion

Every group member can take on one of these roles. Alternating roles gives everyone a chance to try out several of them.

Organizer	Keeps the discussion moving; keeps group on topic; summarizes group's work.
Contributor (one or more)	Adds information to discussion; offers both positive and negative comments.
Peacemaker	Listens and watches group interaction; offers positive statements; settles conflicts among members.
Recorder	Keeps written records of the discussion; writes a summary.
Spokesperson	Speaks for the group; presents discussion summary to the whole class.

Carrying out the responsibilities of the above roles gets every group member actively involved in the discussion. You are actively involved when you . . .

- Ask questions related to the topic.
- Challenge statements of classmates.
- Add more information to what was already said.
- Give your own opinions and use facts or examples as evidence.
- Bring and show objects that relate to the discussion.
- Tell only the relevant part of what you know and don't try to dominate the discussion by going on and on.

Interviewing

Definition: Individuals ask questions of an interviewee to solicit information. Interviewer inquires, listens, gathers information, and condenses it.

Activity Sheets

- page 93
  People Hunt (a get-acquainted interview)

- page 94
  Who Likes What? (a get-acquainted interview)

Circulate among your classmates to complete this people hunt. Gather your information, compare results, and compile one group summary to share with the class.

PEOPLE HUNT

Find a person who . . .

- has two or more TV sets at home.
- can cross his or her eyes.
- has read two or more books this month.
- loves to eat limes.
- has more than six brothers or sisters.
- listens to your favorite radio station.
- has played a team sport.
- can play an instrument.
- has two pets in his or her home.
- has traveled out of the country.

MORE TO DO

BUZZ GROUPS/LISTENING SKILLS
Follow these steps to play "Gossip."

1. Read a short news article about someone famous.
2. Whisper the news to the next person in your buzz group.
3. That person whispers it to the next person, and so on.
4. The last person in the group will report the news aloud to the group.

Discuss your experiment and have one group member report the conclusions of your discussion to the class.

PROCEDURES: Prior to the activity, have students brainstorm several additional "people hunt" statements. Then, each interviewer selects ten "searching statements." Allow less than ten minutes for the interviewing and the group discussions. After this activity, the students will know interesting things about each other.

WHO LIKES WHAT?

1. With the class, brainstorm a list of possible categories for "favorite things." Here are a few suggestions:
   - food
   - clothes
   - TV shows
   - sports

   Make your category list as long as you can.
2. Write interview questions for those categories.
3. Select a classmate and ask him or her your list of interview questions.
4. Introduce your classmate by condensing and sharing with the class the information that you learned through your interview. For example:

   > Our friend's name is Felipe, and his two favorite sports are football and soccer—football to *watch* (especially the San Francisco 49ers), and soccer to *play*. Another favorite activity of his is watching television; Felipe's favorite show is "Miami Vice."
5. After a dozen classmates have been introduced, write your interviewee's name on a sheet of paper.
6. Circulate the paper around the class. Tell each classmate to list one of that person's favorite things on the paper.
7. When the list is complete, the person whose name is on each sheet of paper tells whether the listed information is correct.

MORE TO DO

BUZZ GROUPS/SCIENCE
In buzz groups of five classmates, spend ten minutes discussing your favorite parts of science class. Then each of you writes two of your science favorites on a slip of paper. Within your group, classmates guess who each person is from the two things listed.

PROCEDURES: Monitor the interview sessions and listen for specific questioning techniques.

Buzz Groups

Definition: A method to get a large number of people (meeting in small groups) quickly involved in discussing a problem and generating questions about it.

Activity Sheets

- page 96
  Dinner Menu (a situation for problem solving)
- page 97
  School Problems (a list of problem situations)

Activity Guidelines

- Form groups of five or six students each.
- Give each group a set period of time (from five to ten minutes) for discussion.
- Have a spokesperson from each group report back to the class.

Join a buzz group. Plan a dinner menu for the class. Your group must agree on the menu. List many possibilities. Then, choose one food for each category.

Your goal is to please as many people as possible. Discuss how you could determine if your choices are acceptable to the majority of the class.

DINNER MENU

Include the following:

one main dish

one vegetable

one salad

one dessert

MORE TO DO

ROLE PLAYING
Perform a skit of you and your friends enjoying a class dinner. Demonstrate how each member of the group likes the menu.

PROCEDURES: Use a student-devised method to determine which buzz group's menu is most successful in pleasing the greatest number of people.

A local political leader has asked for your help in dealing with some of the problems that plague schools in this country. Get into buzz groups. Select one problem for discussion.

SCHOOL PROBLEMS

tardiness	drugs
absenteeism	violence
vandalism	drop-outs

Here are some issues to consider:

- Why is it a problem?
- What harm does it cause?
- How many people does it affect?
- Whose responsibility is it?
- What could be done to reduce or eliminate the problem?

Share your decisions in whole-class discussion.

MORE TO DO

ROLE PLAYING
Role play a school problem. Include an occurrence of the problem, a series of events in which you try to solve the problem, and a solution.

PANEL DISCUSSION
Select one school problem and do research on it, using magazines, newspapers, and interviews. Send one member of your group to the panel to represent your group's research.

INTERVIEWING
Interview members of your school community who have been at the school for quite a number of years. Compare school life "then" and "now."

PROCEDURE: Invite the principal to your class to hear the results of the buzz groups.

Brainstorming

Definition: A means of releasing creativity and generating a quantity of ideas about specific problems before the decison-making/problem-solving stage is reached.

Activity Sheets

- page 99
  What in the World! (a cartoon for interpretation)

- page 100
  Problems Aplenty (a list of problem situations)

- page 101
  Myth-Making (creating original myths)

Activity Guidelines

Be sure that students know the ground rules for brainstorming:

- List every idea suggested. No ideas are too wild.
- Don't criticize any ideas, since you are not concerned with validity at this time.
- Go for quantity of ideas; "the more the merrier."
- Go for a chain reaction of ideas. Try to add to, combine, or improve on the ideas of others.

Look at this cartoon. What in the world is going on? In your group, brainstorm a list of ideas to explain what is happening or might happen. Then work with ideas from the list to develop one creative explanation of the cartoon. Pick one group member to tell it to the class.

WHAT IN THE WORLD!

MORE TO DO

DRAWING
Draw your own strange or funny pictures to use for group brainstorming.

BUZZ GROUPS
Cut out comic strips, cutting off the last two frames. For ten minutes, discuss in buzz groups a variety of possible endings to each strip. Then pick the ending that works best. As a challenge, make your own unfinished comic strips.

PROCEDURES: After the class hears all the group explanations, let them pick their favorite one.

Read these problems. Choose one and take turns in your group offering possible solutions. Have a recorder take notes during the brainstorming. After everyone has contributed at least once, discuss the solutions and select the best ones to share with the whole class.

PROBLEMS APLENTY

- Your sister received a mean letter from one of your friends.
- You are tardy and the class is taking a test. You need to convince the teacher to let you take the test.
- A fire-breathing dragon is walking the streets.
- All your friends are staying after school for the pep rally; your mother will get home from work in one hour, and you need her permission to stay.
- Your mother is sick and your father is out of town, so you have to prepare dinner tonight.
- Your sister dropped her triple-scoop ice cream on your new jacket.
- Someone you really like asks to copy your social studies homework.
- Someone left a tiny, straggly kitten outside your door and your parents say "NO."
- You found a wallet on the sidewalk containing three $100 bills.
- An elephant is chasing your brother.

PROCEDURES: Give the groups three minutes to list solutions for a single problem. After the groups share their solutions, let the class select the best one for each problem.

In your group, brainstorm what you think each of these characters from Greek mythology might have done. What were their mythological roles? Then brainstorm ideas for creating your own myth around one or two of the characters. Select one member to tell your myth to the class.

MYTH-MAKING

Greek Name	Mythological Role
Aphrodite	Goddess of love and beauty
Apollo	God of healing, music, and poetry
Athena	Goddess of wisdom and women's crafts
Hestia	Goddess of hearth and home
Zeus	King of the gods
Hebe	God of youth
Morpheus	God of dreams
Iris	Goddess of the rainbow

MORE TO DO

RESEARCH AND REPORTING
Six students can serve as the Hamilton panel experts and use Edith Hamilton's *Mythology* as a resource book. Their job is to report to the class how the group myths compare to the originals.

STORYTELLING
Assign one name of a god or goddess to a group. Each group will practice storytelling within the group and will select one member to tell the story to the class.

READERS' THEATER
Groups can each pick one Greek god or goddess and prepare a readers' theater script of the myth about that deity. Perform your scripts for the class.

IMPROVISATION
Perform group improvisational skits of some of the Greek myths.

PROCEDURES: This is a good review activity after you have taught the Greek gods and goddesses. Tape the telling of the myths to the class.

Round Table Discussion

Definition: Sharing ideas and dealing with problems in an informal manner in a group of three to eight members with a moderator who guides the discussion, keeps the participants on topic, and summarizes and evaluates the results.

Activity Sheets

- page 103
  Pandora (a Greek myth)

- page 105
  Group Grades (a readers' theater script)

Read this version of the Greek myth about Pandora. When everyone in your round table group is finished, discuss these questions:

1. How would you have stopped Pandora from opening the box?
2. What made Pandora finally lift the lid?
3. What do Pandora's actions mean to us today?
4. Do you think Hope is alive and well in our world today?

Give a group report on your discussion to the class.

PANDORA

Retold by Mary Young Williams

Zeus rumbled and roared. Fire had always been a special treasure of the gods, and now Prometheus had stolen fire for man. Prometheus meant no harm to the gods. He had created man superior to the animals, making them upright so that they could look at the heavens instead of the ground. Because he cared so much about his creation, Prometheus gave man fire for cooking, for warmth, and for defense.

Now Zeus was angry at Prometheus, and also angry at man for accepting the stolen gift of fire. He vowed that man should be punished. His idea for punishment involved the creation of the first woman. When Zeus assembled his gods together, they blessed this woman with gifts such as beauty, wit, charm, and grace, as well as deceit, cunning, and curiosity. They named her Pandora, which means "Gifts of All."

A messenger delivered Pandora to earth and presented her to Epimetheus, the brother of Prometheus. As her dowry from the gods, Pandora carried a golden box, which she had been warned not to open. Although Prometheus had warned his brother against accepting any gifts from the gods, Epimetheus embraced the beautiful maiden, Pandora, and married her that very evening.

Overwhelmed with love and awe, Epimetheus disregarded his brother's warning and prepared a beautiful home for Pandora. Because the beauty of the golden box brought happiness to those who gazed upon it, Epimetheus could not discard it. He rested the box on the table where it glistened in the sunlight each day. Still, Epimetheus cautioned Pandora to heed the warning of the gods and to leave the box unopened.

(continued on the next page)

Each day Pandora stared wistfully at the golden box and wondered about its contents. "A golden robe and precious jewels might be inside! Surely the gods would want me to enhance my beauty, rather than keep such treasures hidden away where no one can enjoy their loveliness."

One day while Epimetheus traveled to visit his brother, Pandora lingered closer and closer to the golden box. With a flash of uncontrollable curiosity, she fingered the latch and then lifted the lid gently to peek at the contents.

With a sudden gush, the lid flew open and hundreds of misty brown, monstrous creatures frolicked and swirled in the air around Pandora. By opening that box, Pandora had released all the evils of mankind—plagues, diease, sorrow, mischief, envy, greed, intolerance, and hatred.

Trying to chase the obnoxious, jeering creatures away, the terrified Pandora fumbled with the latch on the box. Within seconds, she snapped the lid closed, just in time to prevent one broken-winged Hope from escaping. She lifted Hope out of the box and held it close to her heart, where it still remains. Although the evils escaped to invade the entire earth, Hope lives in the heart of all mankind.

MORE TO DO

STORYTELLING AND RESEARCH
Look in mythology books to find different versions of the Pandora myth. Look for myth collections from these authors: Edith Hamilton, Sir James George Grazer, Olivia E. Coolidge, Thomas Bulfinch, and Sally Benson. Tell your group one of the other versions.

BUZZ GROUPS
After collecting several versions of the Pandora myth, work in buzz groups for fifteen minutes to compare them. Do they all make the same point?

PROCEDURES: Before the groups begin the round table discussions, you may want them to engage in some preliminary brainstorming to get a lot of ideas out for discussion. After the group reports, let the class reach some consensus on the four questions.

Use this script for a readers' theater presentation. After the presentation, meet in round table discussion groups. Look at the script and decide which role each character has taken on. Defend your choices with specific examples from the script.

GROUP GRADES

Characters: Chris, Sara, Gabriel, Mary, Jake
Possible Roles in Discussion: Organizer, Contributor, Peacemaker, Recorder, Spokesperson

Sara: What does Mrs. Bukowski want us to do?
Chris: Weren't you listening? She wants us to talk about how she should grade us for our discussion groups. Can you believe it—we actually get a chance to tell her how to grade us! Any ideas?
Gabriel: OK—I've got one. The teacher gives A's just to those people she sees talking.
Sara: Wait! That's not fair. Some of us might talk when she's not looking.
Gabriel: She'd know I was talking. I'd tell her!
Jake: Sure you would, Gabriel, you and 20 others. And things would get out of hand!
Sara: No, I think that's a good idea. Let's write it down.
Chris: Here's a pencil, Jake. Now, any other ideas?
Mary: Look, I'm the one who has to talk to the class! What do you want me to say?
Sara: Don't panic, we haven't settled on anything yet.
Chris: Here's another idea—let everyone in the group get the same grade.
Gabriel: You mean I'd get the same grade as Mary? No fair! She never talks!
Mary: I do too! Just because I'm not a motor-mouth like *some* people!
Sara: Calm down—you're *both* important to the group.
Jake: Wait. What did you say? You guys go too fast for me!
Chris: I'm just thinking, if everybody in the group gets the same grade, we'll all work together, instead of each person trying to show off for the teacher.
Mary: Maybe you're right. If we know we're all going to get the same grade, everyone in the group would *have* to talk.
Gabriel: Hey, did anybody study for the math test?
Mary: We can't spend time talking about the math test! We've got to finish this on time. We'll flunk if we don't finish.
Jake: You know—that's another good reason for giving one grade to the whole group. It will make everyone pay attention and keep to the point so we finish on time—otherwise we'll all get a bad grade.

Mary: Yeah, we'll all get D's because Gabriel's studying math.
Sara: No, he isn't. He's working just as hard as the rest of us.
Chris: If we want to get a decent grade on *this* group discussion, we'd better get to work and think of more ideas.
Mary: Why do we need any more? Let's talk about sharing the same grade. Is that the idea you want me to tell the class?
Jake: Hold it. My notes show that so far we have two ideas—we said you get an A if you talk, or everyone in the group gets the same grade.
Sara: I liked the first idea better.
Chris: That's fine, but we only have a couple of minutes left. We need to plan our report, and we have the most ideas to defend everybody getting the same grade.
Gabriel: It makes sense—a team grade would give us team spirit!
Sara: Yeah, that's right. We'll work together, just like the players on a basketball team.
Gabriel: But what about the freeloaders? Someone might get a good grade even if he didn't talk!
Sara: Naw, that wouldn't happen! No one wants to feel left out. Everyone will talk!
Chris: Mary, you need to sound organized.
Mary: Let me use the notes, Jake.
Chris: Let's go over our idea again. We want all group members to share the same grade. Here's why: (1) We'd work as a team. (2) We'd pay attention better. (3) We'd finish on time. (4) We'd share a team spirit. (5) We'd all want to talk. And (6), a group grade would discourage freeloaders.
Gabriel: I'm not so sure about that last one.
Sara: If someone brings up the freeloader problem, let the class discuss it.
Mary: OK, I guess I'm ready! Wish me luck!
Sara: Good job, everybody!

MORE TO DO

BRAINSTORMING

Offer more opinions about how discussion groups should be given grades. After compiling a list, choose one solution and prepare a list of reasons to defend it.

ROLE PLAYING

Put the script aside and perform role-playing skits in which you discuss other solutions. Talk about the roles different people play in the discussion.

PROCEDURES: Use Guide Sheet 4, page 91, for descriptions of the roles. After five fluent readers read the readers' theater script, hold a class dicussion about the qualities of an effective group.

Panel Discussion

Definition: A discussion format similar to round table but more formal, with three to twelve members who sit on a panel as authorities and hold a public discussion about a problem, then invite the audience to get involved afterwards.

Activity Sheets

- page 108
  Peculiarsome Abe (a biographical excerpt)
- page 109
  Scholarship Giveaway (choosing among applicants)
- page 110
  Agree or Disagree? (a list of opinions for discussion)

Activity Guidelines

- Select members for the panels from buzz groups or brainstorming groups.
- Both panel members and the audience should listen attentively while discussion is going on.
- Suggest that panel members make notes of any statements they want to add to or challenge.

Compare the information in this story from a book about Abe Lincoln with the facts you have learned about Lincoln from history books. Brainstorm a list of those facts with your group. Then select one group member to join a panel that will discuss the differences between the "history book" version and the story version of Abe Lincoln.

PECULIARSOME ABE

from *Abe Lincoln Grows Up*
by Carl Sandburg

The farm boys in their evenings at Jones's store in Gentryville talked about how Abe Lincoln was always reading, digging into books, stretching out flat on his stomach in front of the fireplace, studying till midnight and past midnight, picking a piece of charcoal to write on the fire shovel, shaving off what he wrote, and then writing more— till midnight and past midnight. The next thing Abe would be reading books between the plow handles, it seemed to them. And once trying to speak a last word, Dennis Hanks said, "There's suthin' peculiarsome about Abe."

He wanted to learn, to know, to live, to reach out; he wanted to satisfy hungers and thirsts he couldn't tell about, this big boy of the backwoods. And some of what he wanted so much, so deep down, seemed to be in the books. Maybe in books he would find the answers to dark questions pushing around in the pools of his thoughts and the drifts of his mind. He told Dennis and the other people, "The things I want to know are in books; my best friend is the man who'll git me a book I ain't read." And sometimes friends answered, "Well, books ain't as plenty as wildcats in this part of Indianny."

MORE TO DO

CREATIVE DRAMATICS/SOCIAL STUDIES
Pantomime parts of Lincoln's life; for example, early days in the log cabin, becoming a lawyer, making the Gettysburg Address.

CHORAL READING/SOCIAL STUDIES
Bring in poems or literary works that contain information about Lincoln. Work in groups to prepare a medley of these writings in script form. Share it with the class as a choral reading.

DEBATES/SOCIAL STUDIES
In your group, talk about Lincoln's debates with Stephen Douglas over the issue of slavery. Prepare to recreate the debate for the class. The class will later decide which group presented the most convincing, realistic debate.

PROCEDURES: Focus the discussion with a few questions: What is the purpose of each form? What is literary license? What can a story tell that a textbook cannot, and vice versa?

The parents of an athlete who died young have set up a four-year scholarship in their son's memory. Your group must reach a consensus decision about which of the five applicants below should get the scholarship this year. All five need it in order to go to college, but only **one** can be selected. After you have made your choice, send one member of your group to a panel to tell which person you selected and to give reasons defending your selection.

SCHOLARSHIP GIVEAWAY

Applicants

1. A very active student who is president of the student body and has maintained a B+ grade-point average. Her parents have limited funds because they are paying for an older son to go to college.
2. A very popular student who has a B average. He has a medical condition that keeps him in a wheelchair. Since his family needs so much money for his medical expenses, they cannot afford to send him to college.
3. A straight-A student who lives with her aunt and uncle because her parents were killed in an automobile accident. Her parents did not leave an insurance policy, and her aunt and uncle have five children of their own to educate.
4. A star athlete who was voted Most Valuable Player by the school's athletic league. He has applied for three different athletic scholarships because he wants to be sure he gets one. He is an only child in a single-parent family and he maintains a B– average.
5. A very talented writer who has had her poetry and short stories published in newspapers and magazines. She maintains an A average. Her father is self-employed, and she has ten brothers and sisters.

MORE TO DO

GROUP DISCUSSION/EVALUATION

Discuss and evaluate the panel on the applicants.

1. How often did panel members fail to back up their group's choice with reasons?
2. Were all panel members actively involved in the discussion?
3. Did panel members speak with authority?
4. Did panel members listen to all other opinions attentively?
5. How well did the panel respond to audience questions?

PROCEDURES: Give each group about twenty minutes to discuss the applicants, make their choices, and brainstorm reasons why they picked that person over the others. Each panel member must be ready to give his or her group's reasons during the panel discussion. Have the class audience play Devil's Advocate and challenge the choices.

Your group should select one of these opinions and decide whether you agree or disagree with it. Then brainstorm as many reasons as you can to defend your group's position. Set up your group for a panel discussion and select one reason to elaborate on when you make your presentation to the class.

AGREE OR DISAGREE?

- Boys are smarter than girls.
- Girls are smarter than boys.
- Teachers are a student's best friend.
- Cartoons have too much violence.
- Rock music should be allowed in school.
- A longer lunch period is needed at school.

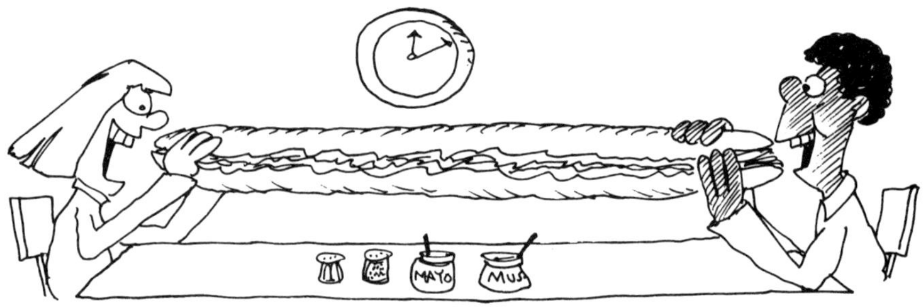

MORE TO DO

PANEL DISCUSSIONS

Here are some additional topics for panel discussion. Take one opinion at a time and discuss all the different views the panels give for or against it.

- Students should have a radio station on campus.
- Age thirteen is too young to start dating.
- A friend should always be totally honest with you.

BUZZ GROUPS

For variety, two groups should choose the same opinion to discuss for a few minutes. When the groups report their results to the class, compare to see how the ideas differ.

ROLE PLAYING

Have each group prepare a role-playing skit based on one of these opinions and share it with the class.

PROCEDURES: Have each group work with a different opinion. After each panel's presentation, discuss whether the panel members defended their positions well enough. If not, was there a problem with students' delivery, or did the problem stem from inadequate brainstorming prior to the panel discussion?

Role-Play Analysis

Definition: A large group or class discussion and analysis of the outcomes presented in role-play enactments as a means of understanding and evaluating other points of view.

Activity Sheets

- page 112
  All in the Family (some common family problems)
- page 113
  Who, What, and Why? (a cartoon for interpretation)
- page 114
  School Days (some decision-making situations)

Activity Guidelines

- Plan role-play situations that progress from simple to more complex.
- Help the audience observe the role playing intelligently by suggesting that they take notes and use checklists.
- When it seems appropriate, have students reenact a role-playing situation after changing or placing audience members in some of the roles for the purpose of clarifying issues and outcomes.
- Have students analyze and compare different outcomes for the same role-play situation in order to determine which outcome is "best" and why.

Work with one of these family problems at a time. Divide into groups and let each group role play the problem and present a solution. Then, as a class, analyze the different outcomes. Follow the six-step method below to choose the best solution. Then go on to the next problem and follow the same procedure.

ALL IN THE FAMILY

- Son doesn't do his homework.
- Mother and father fight over bills.
- Daughter comes home late from school.
- Son and daughter want a later curfew.
- Sister tattles on her younger brother.

STEPS FOR ROLE-PLAY ANALYSIS

1. Identify the problem.
2. Decide what questions need to be asked about the problem.
3. List the possible ways of solving the problem that were offered in the role plays.
4. Repeat some of the enactments if needed to clarify issues.
5. Choose which of these alternatives might really solve the problem. Cross out the ones that would not.
6. Select the one solution that is best, allowing both sides to "win." Give reasons for your choice.

MORE TO DO

BRAINSTORMING
Work in groups to brainstorm other kinds of problems that could be solved through role playing and analysis.

ROUND TABLE DISCUSSION/SCIENCE
Pick a scientific problem and have each group hold a round table discussion to form hypotheses about causes and solutions. For example, the problem might be new viruses that come into the country each year. What might be the cause? What could be done about it? The groups should share their hypotheses with the class. Compile a list of possible causes and solutions; decide which ones sound more realistic.

PROCEDURES: Work with the class as they go through the six-step method outlined on the activity sheet. Use some or all of the family problems listed. Let students add others of their own.

Look at this picture with your group. List possible problems it might be about. Choose one of your ideas and write it in the space below. Then brainstorm and list strategies for solving the problem. Each group should role play its problem and one of the solution strategies. The other groups observe the role play and analyze it.

WHO, WHAT, AND WHY?

What is the problem?

What are some possible strategies for solving it?

Strategy 1:

Strategy 2:

Strategy 3:

MORE TO DO

ROLE PLAYING AND ANALYSIS
Groups can role play situations about other pictures they find in magazines and newspapers. Analyze these enactments, too.

ROLE PLAYING AND ANALYSIS/SCIENCE
Get into small groups to role play doing an experiment in the science classroom. The rest of the class should analyze each enactment to see if the steps followed are correct, complete, and safe.

PROCEDURES: Divide the class into three large groups. Review the six steps for role-play analysis (page 112) as needed.

In your group, select one of the situations below to discuss and role play. Follow the five steps for decision making. Then present a role-playing skit to the class. They will analyze the skit and evaluate your decision to see if you made the best possible choice.

SCHOOL DAYS

- You are on a committee that volunteered to help decide on a new grading system at the school. The present grading system excludes too many students from the honor roll.
- You are a new student at school and have just learned about the rule that says you will be suspended if you leave campus. A class officer that you have admired asks you to go to a fast-food restaurant to get lunch, and you don't know anyone else to have lunch with.
- You have to write an essay that will be worth one-fourth of your semester grade. You want to write the best essay you have ever done, but you put off writing it until the last night. A good friend asks you to go to a party that night with a popular classmate you have been trying to meet.

STEPS FOR DECISION MAKING

1. Identify what decision has to be made.
2. List possible choices for the decision.
3. Discuss the pros and cons of each choice.
4. Talk to others who could help with making the decision.
5. Make your decision based on all the information you have collected.

MORE TO DO

BUZZ GROUPS
Work in small groups for ten minutes to discuss other problems that might arise at school and think about possible decisions.

BRAINSTORMING AND PANEL DISCUSSION
Brainstorm in groups some of the things you might do to take care of your school. Follow the five decision-making steps to pick two or three. Send a spokesperson to join a panel to discuss suggestions and to make a list for the class to follow.

PROCEDURES: Read all three situations aloud to the groups before they begin, and go over the five decision-making steps with them. Help the class analyze each role-playing skit, following the six steps for role-play analysis (page 112)

Spin-Offs

Interviewing

- Have each student select someone in the school community and write up the results of the interview in the form of a human-interest news story, as if for *People* magazine. The best of these stories could be submitted to your school or community newspaper, or you could collect them as a "Who's Who at (Name) School."
- Students might conduct opinion polls within the school on subjects of their choice. Require that they interview a cross-section of students and teachers, not just their own friends.

Buzz Groups

- Have students use buzz group skills to organize team competitions for reviewing materials in various content areas. This is an extremely good way for them to review for tests.

Brainstorming

- Give students newspapers to use in brainstorming groups to search for discussion topics that could serve as a basis for round table discussions, panel discussions, and role-play analysis.
- Have students brainstorm ways that familiar fairy tales and nursery rhymes could be changed to make them reflect the modern world. They can prepare some of these for a "Modern Mother Goose" presentation that includes puppets, story theater, and choral reading.

Round Table

- Use round table discussions to promote vocabulary development. Each group chooses one abstract word, such as *love, hate, joy,* or *sadness.* In their discussion, they are to explore ways to express the abstraction in more concrete terms. You might suggest that they use a thesaurus and children's literature books to look for synonyms. The result of the discussion should be a list of 20 sentences that give concrete examples of the abstract word's meaning; for example, "Love is a kiss on a tear-stained cheek after I scrape my knee." Each round table group should decide on a way to present the results of their discussion to the class, perhaps through a role-playing skit, a choral reading, or a panel discussion.

Panel Discussion

- Let students hold panel discussion about controversial matters in the sports world. Here are some questions to get them started.
    - Should college sports stars have to get good grades?
    - How high should the salaries go for professional players?
    - Should the government pay the way for our Olympic teams?
    - Should teams be made up of both men and women?

Role-Play Analysis

- Prepare index cards with "What would you do?" problem situations on them, one per card, to use throughout the year for group discussion and role play and analysis situations.
- To increase reading comprehension, ask students to do role playing based on characters and situations in literature they are reading together in class.

GROUP DISCUSSION
Rating Sheet 1

Your name ______________________________ Date ______________

P = Poor
A = Average
C = Clever
E = Exceptional

RATE YOURSELF
Find your group discussion PACE rating.

GROUP WORK: You . . .	P	A	C	E
interacted cooperatively with everyone.				
learned and used group task roles.				
actively contributed to discussions.				
gave others their turns to give opinions.				
showed interest in other opinions.				
made decisions.				
helped keep the discussions orderly.				
followed directions.				

GETTING READY: You . . .	P	A	C	E
took part in planning and organizing the discussions.				
thought through ideas to use in discussions.				
prepared notes, found materials to back up opinions.				
practiced being poised and composed when speaking.				
considered others' ideas for discussion topics.				
planned the use of time.				

DISCUSSION: You . . .	P	A	C	E
were articulate when speaking.				
showed increased ability to use language.				
listened critically.				
identified, organized, summarized, evaluated concepts.				
analyzed and solved problems.				
supported opinions with reasons, examples, and facts.				
stayed with the topic under discussion.				
encouraged differing points of view.				

Comment on what you did best in group discussion.

Comment on what was hardest for you.

What changes would you make the next time?

Classmate's name ______________________ Date ____________

RATE A CLASSMATE
Find the group discussion PACE rating for a classmate in your group.

P = Poor
A = Average
C = Clever
E = Exceptional

GROUP WORK: This classmate . . .	P	A	C	E
interacted cooperatively with everyone.				
learned and used group task roles.				
actively contributed to discussions.				
gave others their turns to give opinions.				
showed interest in other opinions.				
made decisions.				
helped keep the discussions orderly.				
followed directions.				

GETTING READY: This classmate . . .	P	A	C	E
took part in planning and organizing the discussions.				
thought through ideas to use in discussions.				
prepared notes, found materials to back up opinions.				
practiced being poised and composed when speaking.				
considered others' ideas for discussion topics.				
planned the use of time.				

DISCUSSION: This classmate . . .	P	A	C	E
was articulate when speaking.				
showed increased ability to use language.				
listened critically.				
identified, organized, summarized, evaluated concepts.				
analyzed and solved problems.				
supported opinions with reasons, examples, and facts.				
stayed with the topic under discussion.				
encouraged differing points of view.				

Comment on what your classmate did best in group discussion.

Comment on what seemed hardest for your classmate.

What changes would you suggest the next time?

Your name ______________________

GROUP DISCUSSION
Rating Sheet 3

Names of Group Members

Date ______________

______________ ______________
______________ ______________
______________ ______________

P = Poor
A = Average
C = Clever
E = Exceptional

RATE YOUR GROUP
Find your group discussion PACE rating.

GROUP WORK: The group members . . .

	P	A	C	E
interacted cooperatively with everyone.				
learned and used group task roles.				
actively contributed to discussions.				
gave others their turns to give opinions.				
showed interest in other opinions.				
made decisions.				
helped keep the discussions orderly.				
followed directions.				

GETTING READY: The group members . . .

	P	A	C	E
took part in planning and organizing the discussions.				
thought through ideas to use in discussions.				
prepared notes, found materials to back up opinions.				
practiced being poised and composed when speaking.				
considered others' ideas for discussion topics.				
planned the use of time.				

DISCUSSION: The group members . . .

	P	A	C	E
were articulate when speaking.				
showed increased ability to use language.				
listened critically.				
identified, organized, summarized, evaluated concepts.				
analyzed and solved problems.				
supported opinions with reasons, examples, and facts.				
stayed with the topic under discussion.				
encouraged differing points of view.				

Comment on what your group did best in group discussion.

Comment on what was hardest for your group.

What changes would you make the next time?

Your name ______________

Appendix A
A Continuum of Oral Language Skills

Looking over a skills continuum may give you a sense of where to begin. However, please don't feel limited by such a list. Like elastic, these skills can stretch this way and that. I encourage you to try any and all of these oral language skills at the appropriate level of difficulty for the grade you are teaching. Use them with the activities in *Let 'Em Talk* to meet the oral language requirements of your school district.

Grades K–4

Sharing information
Giving directions
Following directions
Giving explanations
Following explanations
Taking part in conversations
Talking over the phone
Making announcements and reports
Making introductions
Discussing recordings, television, and other media
Restating announcements made over the intercom system
Retelling stories
Discussing stories and poetry
Discussing dramatizations
Reading orally with emphasis on intonation
Reciting poetry, rhymes, and jingles
Participating in choral speaking
Participating in finger play
Participating in improvisations
Participating in book talks
Using puppets

Grades 5–8

Predicting story endings
Taking part in conversations
Talking over the phone
Speaking in choral groups
Participating in discussions
Participating in interviews
Making announcements
Making introductions
Giving explanations
Telling original stories
Reading stories orally
Reading poems orally
Dramatizing stories
Giving informal talks
Making oral reports
Making tape recordings
Participating in television programs
Discussing films and other media
Participating in storytelling
Participating in readers' theater
Participating in group discussions
Delivering formal speeches
Participating in panel discussions

Appendix B
The Teacher's Role and Lesson Planning

Think about how you have the power to affect the lives of so many! The successes of your students reflect *your* confidence, philosophy, and curriculum goals. Yours is a power that I respect, for I know that you control the effectiveness of this book. You decide whether you browse through it or *use* it. Oral language skills will just stagnate between these pages until you energize the words and ideas; nothing will happen unless you provoke your students into interaction and "let 'em talk." I invite you to examine your role in oral language development in light of my ideas on teaching style and lesson planning. Then— set the stage for your students, give them a stimulating environment, and enjoy yourself.

Teaching Style

Think about YOU.

WHAT YOU ARE . . .
- a motivator
- a facilitator
- an organizer
- a stimulator
- a leader

WHAT YOU HAVE . . .
- patience
- curiosity
- a spirit of adventure
- sensitivity
- enthusiasm

WHAT YOU DO . . .
- listen
- read aloud
- ask questions
- give feedback
- offer new experiences
- plan repeat experiences

Think about your interactive classroom.

The teacher provides . . .
- information.
- opportunities for speaking.
- materials.
  - verse
  - pattern books.
  - wordless books.
  - folktales and fables.
  - models from literature.
- various audiences.
- equipment.
- problem-solving situations.
- strategies for group work.

→

The students respond by . . .
- interacting.
- reading aloud.
- cooperating.
- performing together.
- talking about themselves.
- brainstorming.
- discussing.
- interviewing.
- evaluating oral messages.
- persuading one another.
- role playing.
- expressing thoughts.

Lesson Planning

The real success of this book hinges on your ability to look beyond its pages and plan your own oral language activities. The bibliography helps you select literature models; this section encourages you to plan oral language lessons that exercise the students' higher-level thinking skills.

An effective teacher plans activities to translate curriculum so that students gain not only knowledge but also social skills and information-processing skills. When students can process content, you have given them a powerful lifelong gift.

Below and on the following page are six lists of verbs that generally coincide with each of six levels of thinking (which you may recognize from Bloom's taxonomy). Using these verbs helps you write lessons to draw on and enhance the innate abilities of your students.

To plan an activity, think of the speaking skill you would like to develop, and then write an objective that builds on one of the listed verbs. Challenge yourself to go beyond knowledge and comprehension and plan activities that develop the higher-level thinking skills of analysis and synthesis.

1. Knowledge

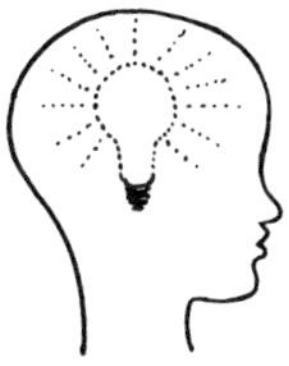

draw
list
write
point
recall
recognize
select
identify
define
locate
name/label

Role: Teacher directs, tells, shows, examines.

2. Comprehension

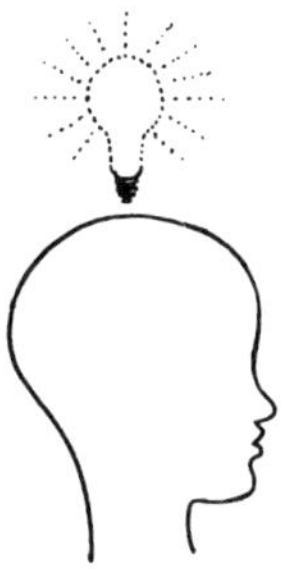

distinguish
restate
associate
rewrite
compare
express
describe
infer
discuss
classify
relate
contrast
predict
convert

Role: Teacher demonstrates, listens, questions, compares, contrasts, examines.

3. Application

apply
calculate
dramatize
classify
employ
modify
examine
illustrate
produce
practice
choose
use
solve
prepare
relate
change

Role: Teacher shows, facilitates, observes, criticizes.

4. Analysis

analyze
detect
survey
explain
categorize
differentiate
infer
subdivide
order
relate
select
separate
transform
summarize
distinguish

Role: Teacher probes, guides, observes.

5. Synthesis

arrange
compose
combine
plan
prepare
invent
construct
role play
design
create
originate
develop
hypothesize
revise

Role: Teacher reflects, extends, analyzes, evaluates.

6. Evaluation

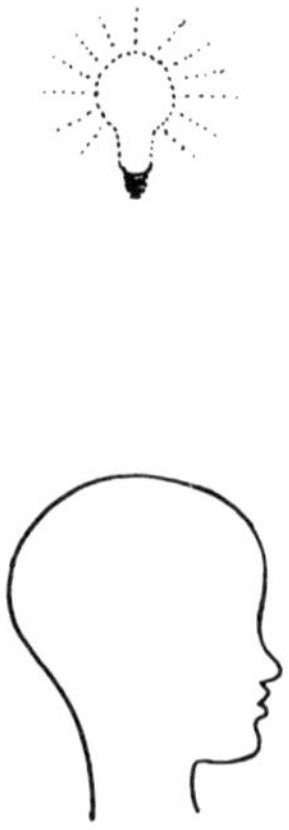

appraise
compare
critique
recommend
determine
weigh
evaluate
criticize
judge
consider
assess
relate
summarize
support

Role: Teacher accepts, harmonizes, appraises.

Bibliography

This bibliography launches you into a world of talking adventures. It includes many of the books I have used as resources for my oral language program. I beg you to go beyond this list. Visit school and public libraries and tap the valuable knowledge and experience of the librarians. Start with the Caldecott and Newbery book lists for outstanding examples of children's literature. Look for Jim Trelease's *The Read-Aloud Handbook* (New York: Penguin Books, 1983), which contains a detailed guide to more than three hundred books that would be excellent for oral language activities.

My greatest discovery came the year I abandoned recommended reading lists and began using children's literature with my class of eighth graders. No, it's *not* beneath them! Question the notion that the truths and emotional impact of *The Giving Tree* or *The Velveteen Rabbit* belong only to the preschooler. Go beyond recommended book lists; pick up any book. If you enjoy it, feel its rhythm, and hear its message, then plan your lessons based on your own instincts for the sound of language. Trust those instincts and you'll breathe new life into your classroom.

With each selection listed here, a suggestion of how it might be used for oral language activities in the classroom appears in parentheses at the end of the annotation. These are only suggestions; as in the other sections of this book, feel free to experiment by shuffling the forms around and adapting any story or poem for different uses.

Aesop's Fables. Retold by Joan Hirschmann. New York: Dell Publishing Co., 1964.

A beautifully illustrated collection of fables, with the wisdom and humor that have survived for centuries. **(storytelling)**

Allard, Harry and James Marshall. *Miss Nelson Is Missing.* Boston: Houghton Mifflin Co., 1977.

A delightful story of school children who miss their teacher and improve their behavior when she returns. **(role playing)**

Andersen, Hans Christian and the Brothers Grimm. *The Best Fairy Tales.* London: Octopus Books Limited, 1984.

Nine familiar stories from the European folk tradition, presented in an illustrated edition. **(improvisation)**

Best Loved Folk-Tales of the World. Selected and with an introduction by Joanna Cole. Garden City, N.Y.: Anchor Press, Doubleday and Company, Inc., 1982.

A comprehensive collection of two hundred varied folktales with a detailed introduction that explores the history of folktales and fairy tales. **(storytelling)**

Butler, Francelia. *Sharing Literature with Children.* New York: David McKay Co., Inc., 1977.

This anthology of children's literature of fantasy and folktales, organized by thematic units and values, is intended to reach or reawaken the "hidden" children in older readers. **(oral interpretation)**

Cameron, Polly. *"I Can't" Said the Ant.* New York: Scholastic Book Services, 1961.

In a book of rhyme, a teapot tells how it is put back together through the cooperation of all the things in the kitchen. **(choral reading)**

A Child's Book of Stories. New York: Children's Classics, a division of Dilithium Press, Ltd., 1986.

Originally published in 1911, this book of stories includes over eighty classics and the illustrations of Jessie Willcox Smith. **(oral interpretation)**

Cuentos, Tales from the Hispanic Southwest. Selected and adapted in Spanish by Jose Griego y Maestas. Retold in English by Rudolfo A. Anaya. Santa Fe, N.M.: The Museum of New Mexico Press, 1980.

Stories, legends, and myths of the Hispanic culture of New Mexico and southern Colorado. Much of the immensely rich folklore is a reflection of the era of Don Quixote. **(storytelling)**

Drummer Hoff. Adapted by Barbara Emberley. Englewood Cliffs, N.J.: Prentice-Hall, Inc., 1967.

A lively folk verse about the building of a cannon. The rhyme and rhythm of the verse encourage a classroom full of chanting. **(chanting)**

Fairy Tale Magic. Newmarket, England: Brimax Books, 1984.

Another outstanding collection of fairy tales. **(improvisation)**

Favorite Nursery Tales. Retold by Morrell Gipson. Garden City, N.Y.: Doubleday and Company, Inc., 1983.

Ten nursery tales with the repetition that appeals to young children. **(story theater)**

The Fisherman and the Magic Fish. Retold by Archie Bennett. Pleasantville, N.Y.: Reader's Digest Services, Inc., 1976.

A new version of the old tale from the Brothers Grimm. A fisherman catches a fish who claims to be a magic prince. The fisherman releases his catch, but his wife sends him back to the sea to ask the magic fish to grant their wishes. **(storytelling)**

Frost, Robert. *Stopping By Woods on a Snowy Evening.* New York: E. P. Dutton, Inc., 1978.

A beautifully illustrated version of the Frost poem. **(choral reading)**

Gag, Wanda. *Millions of Cats.* New York: Coward, McCann and Geoghegan, Inc., 1928.

The classic story of "hundreds of cats, thousands of cats, millions and billions and trillions of cats," and the one cat of all that the older couple chose to live with them. **(choral reading)**

Gauch, Patricia Lee. *Christina Katerina and the Box.* New York: Coward, McCann and Geoghegan, Inc., 1971.

A refrigerator box takes on life because of the imagination of the children. **(group discussion)**

Hadley, Eric and Tessa. *Legends of Earth, Air, Fire, and Water.* New York: Cambridge University Press, 1985.

Legends from the Cree, Aboriginal, Japanese, Iroquois, Polynesian, Italian, Bantu, South American, Finnish, Cameroon, and Chinese, involving the great universal elements—earth, air, fire, and water. **(storytelling)**

Heirloom Classics. Retold by Jane Carruth. Chicago: Rand McNally and Co., 1980.

An illustrated collection of fairy-tale classics with elaborate descriptions and enriched vocabulary. **(readers' theater)**

Hoban, Russell. *Best Friends for Frances.* New York: Scholastic Book Services, 1969.

Two sisters become best friends in this comfortable story and picture book. **(group discussion, role playing)**

Hoberman, Mary Ann. *A House Is a House for Me.* New York: The Viking Press, 1978.

Offers many interpretations of "houses," presented through the rhythmic repetition of "a house is a house for me." Let it stimulate critical thinking and vocabulary development. **(chanting)**

Hume, Lotta Carswell. *Favorite Children's Stories from China and Tibet.* Rutland, Vt.: Charles E. Tuttle Company, 1962.

Nineteen stories from various parts of China and Tibet, with humorous insights into Chinese life. One point of particular interest: the Chinese Cinderella is quite different from the Cinderella tales we inherited from the European tradition. **(storytelling)**

The Illustrated Treasury of Fairy Tales. Edited by T. A. Kennedy. New York: Grosset and Dunlap, Inc., 1982.

Fairy tales interpreted by a succession of classic illustrators. **(creative dramatics)**

Joslin, Sesyle. *What Do You Say, Dear?* New York: Scholastic Book Services, 1958.

This book of manners for all occasions, both comical and adventurous, asks the reader to respond to the familiar motherly question, "What do you say, dear?" **(choral reading)**

Kessler, Ethel and Leonard. *What's Inside the Box?* New York: Firefly Paperbacks, A Scholastic Book Service, 1976.

Several animals try to guess what's inside the box. **(readers' theater)**

Kipling, Rudyard. *The Elephant's Child.* New York: Harcourt Brace Jovanovich, Inc., 1983.

An African pourquoi tale that tells how the elephant got its trunk. The detailed descriptions of the setting and the characters add to the picturesque quality of this tale. **(storytelling)**

Krauss, Ruth. *The Carrot Seed.* New York: Harper and Row, Publishers, 1945.

This picture book shows the determination of a young child who makes a carrot plant grow, even though everyone says it won't. **(pantomime)**

Leodhas, Sorche Nic. *Always Room for One More.* New York: Holt, Rinehart and Winston, Inc. 1965.

A Scottish tale of Lachie MacLachlan, who lives in his "wee house in the heather" with his family of twelve and welcomes any weary traveler who passes by on a stormy night. Soon his house bulges at the seams with joy. **(storytelling)**

Lisker, Sonia. *I Used To.* New York: Four Winds Press, 1977.

Six-year-olds think about things they "used to" believe and do. Use this to stimulate personal sharing. **(choral reading, buzz groups)**

Lobel, Arnold. *Frog and Toad Are Friends.* New York: Harper and Row, Publishers, 1977.

The stories of Frog and Toad are packed with gaiety, adventure, and affection. **(creative dramatics)**

Mayer, Mercer. *If I Had . . .* New York: The Dial Press, 1968.

A boy dreams of defending himself against bullies. This refreshing story shows the love for an older brother. **(role playing)**

———. *Frog, Where Are You?* New York: The Dial Press, 1969.

The creative dialogue of children is stimulated as they put their own words into this wordless book. **(improvisation)**

———. *What Do You Do with a Kangaroo?* New York: Scholastic Book Services, 1973.

With the repeating query of "What do you do?" children are asked to solve the problems created when various animals come to visit. **(readers' theater)**

The Mitten. Retold by Alvin Tresselt. New York: Scholastic, Inc., 1964.

Many forest animals find shelter in a boy's lost mitten in this old Ukrainian cumulative folktale with good dialogue and colorful detail. **(storytelling)**

The Old Fashioned Storybook. Selections by Betty Ann Schwartz and Leon Archibald. New York: A Little Simon Book, Simon and Schuster, Inc., 1985.

A beautifully illustrated collection of twenty classic tales, including work from the Brothers Grimm, Hans Christian Andersen, Rudyard Kipling, Charles Perrault, Oscar Wilde, and tales from Russia, Poland, England, and Norway. **(storytelling)**

Preston, Edna Mitchell. *Squawk to the Moon, Little Goose.* New York: Scholastic Book Services, 1974.

A goose runs to the farmer to tell him about the disappearing moon and chants, "Good's good and bad's bad. I must go tell the farmer." The goose nearly runs afoul of a fox, but is saved when the fox is convinced that the moon's reflection in the pond is cheese. **(choral reading)**

The Random House Book of Poetry for Children. Selected and introduced by Jack Prelutsky. New York: Random House, 1983.

An assortment of excellent poems to stimulate creative thinking and participation in oral language activities. **(oral interpretation)**

Rico, Ulde. *The Rainbow Goblins.* New York: Warner Books, Inc., 1983.

The landscape of the rainbow goblins snares the reader in picturesque detail. Use this excellent book for vocabulary development and appreciation of details. **(readers' theater)**

Ruck-Pauquet, Gina. *Mumble Bear.* New York: G. P. Putnam's Sons, 1980.

A kind bear who helps other animals and never takes time for himself mumbles about not doing the things he likes. In the end, he does what he wants and finds out he still has planty of friends. **(group discussion)**

Rusling, Albert. *The Mouse and Mrs. Proudfoot.* Englewood Cliffs, N.J.: Prentice-Hall, Inc., 1984.

The attempts of Mrs. Proudfoot to get rid of a mouse sparkle with humor in this cumulative tale. **(storytelling)**

Sendak, Maurice. *Pierre.* New York: Scholastic Book Services, 1962.

A boy constantly says, "I don't care!" Though it is short, the book contains five chapters and a prologue and gives children a sense of story structure. **(readers' theater)**

———. *Chicken Soup with Rice.* New York: Scholastic Book Services, 1962.

This book of months contains excellent refrains for oral language activities. **(chanting)**

———. *Where the Wild Things Are.* New York: Harper and Row, Publishers, 1963.

In a modern classic that every child understands, Max confronts the wild things in his dreams. **(story theater)**

Seuss, Dr. [Theodore S. Geisel]. *Horton Hatches the Egg.* New York: Random House, 1968.

A helpful elephant promises to sit on a bird's egg until it hatches. All the books of Dr. Seuss have a powerful rhythm, which makes them especially suitable for oral language activities. **(readers' theater)**

Silverstein, Shel. *The Giving Tree.* New York: Harper and Row, Publishers, 1964.

A tree gives and gives and gives to a boy as he grows to be a man. The story offers many abstract concepts for discussion, such as the "journey of man" and living with the givers and takers of the world. **(round table or panel discussion)**

——— *Where the Sidewalk Ends.* New York: Harper and Row, Publishers, 1977.

Wonderfully humorous poetry on topics for young people. Always popular for oral language activities. **(oral interpretation)**

Slobodkina, Esphyr. *Caps for Sale.* New York: Scholastic, Inc., 1968.

A peddler, some monkeys, and some monkey business lead to adventure. Children can chant the colors of the caps. **(chanting)**

Smith, Jessie Willcox. *The Jessie Willcox Smith Mother Goose.* New York: Derrydale Books, 1986.

A beautifully illustrated collection of Mother Goose, with historical background about the original rhymes. **(creative dramatics)**

Stoutenburg, Adrien. *American Tall Tales.* New York: Penguin Books, 1966.

Tales of America's colorful folk heroes, including Paul Bunyan, Pecos Bill, Stormalong, Mike Fink, Davy Crockett, Johnny Appleseed, and John Henry. **(storytelling)**

Tigers and Opposums, Animal Legends. Adapted by Marcos Kurtycz and Ana Garcia Kobeh. Boston: Little, Brown and Co., 1984.

Six Mexican folktales capture a world where animals speak. **(storytelling)**

Viorst, Judith. *Alexander and the Terrible, Horrible, No Good, Very Bad Day.* Hartford, Conn.: Connecticut Printers, Inc., 1972.

A series of comical situations in the life of Alexander help us understand that everyone sometimes has a bad day. **(readers' theater)**

Vogel, Ilse-Margaret. *The Don't Be Scared Book.* New York: Atheneum Publishers, 1964.

A pattern book with comical cures for fears that many children share. **(pantomime)**

Walt Disney's Treasury of Children's Classics. Edited by Darlene Geis. New York: Harry N. Abrams, Inc., 1978.

Fairy tales, classics, and contemporary stories, adapted from the Disney motion picture productions. **(oral interpretation)**

Why Corn Is Golden: Stories About Plants. Adapted by Vivien Blackmore. Boston: Little, Brown and Co., 1984.

Pourquoi stories from the Mexican Indians, from the days when people worshiped the elements: rain, sun, wind, fire. **(storytelling)**

Williams, Margery. *The Velveteen Rabbit.* New York: A Little Simon Book, Simon and Schuster, Inc., 1983.

A boy's love for a velveteen rabbit makes it come to life. **(group discussion)**